A Framework For Understanding Poverty

The mission of **aha!** Process, Inc. is to positively impact the education and lives of individuals in poverty around the world.

Payne, Ruby K.
    A Framework for Understanding Poverty. Revised edition, 80 pp.
    Bibliography pp. 77-79
    ISBN 09647437-0-1

1. Education   2. Sociology   3. Title

Other selected titles by Ruby K. Payne, Ph.D.

A Framework for Understanding Poverty
Un Marco Para Entender la Pobreza
Understanding Learning
Learning Structures
Preventing School Violence by Creating Emotional Safety: Video Series & Manual
Meeting Standards & Raising Test Scores
        When you don't have much time or money – Video Series & Manual (Payne & Magee)
Removing the Mask: Giftedness in Poverty (Slocumb & Payne)
Bridges Out of Poverty: *Strategies for Professionals and Communities* (Payne, Devol & Smith)
Think Rather of Zebra (Stailey & Payne)
What Every Church Member Should Know About Poverty (Payne & Ehlig)
Living on a Tightrope – a Survival Handbook for Principals (Payne & Sommers)
Hidden Rules of Class at Work (Payne & Krabill)

Ruby K. Payne. Ph.D.

A Framework For Understanding Poverty

C*ontents*

MODULE ONE

OVERVIEW AND STATISTICS:
KEY POINTS

Workshop Objectives

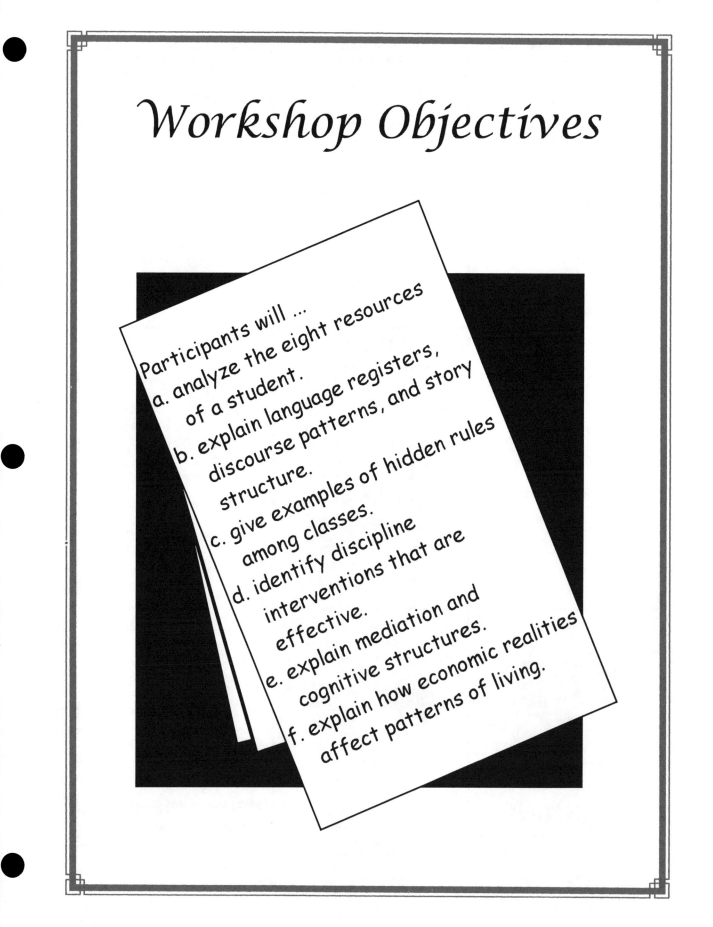

Participants will ...
a. analyze the eight resources of a student.
b. explain language registers, discourse patterns, and story structure.
c. give examples of hidden rules among classes.
d. identify discipline interventions that are effective.
e. explain mediation and cognitive structures.
f. explain how economic realities affect patterns of living.

aha! Process, Inc. • (800) 424-9484

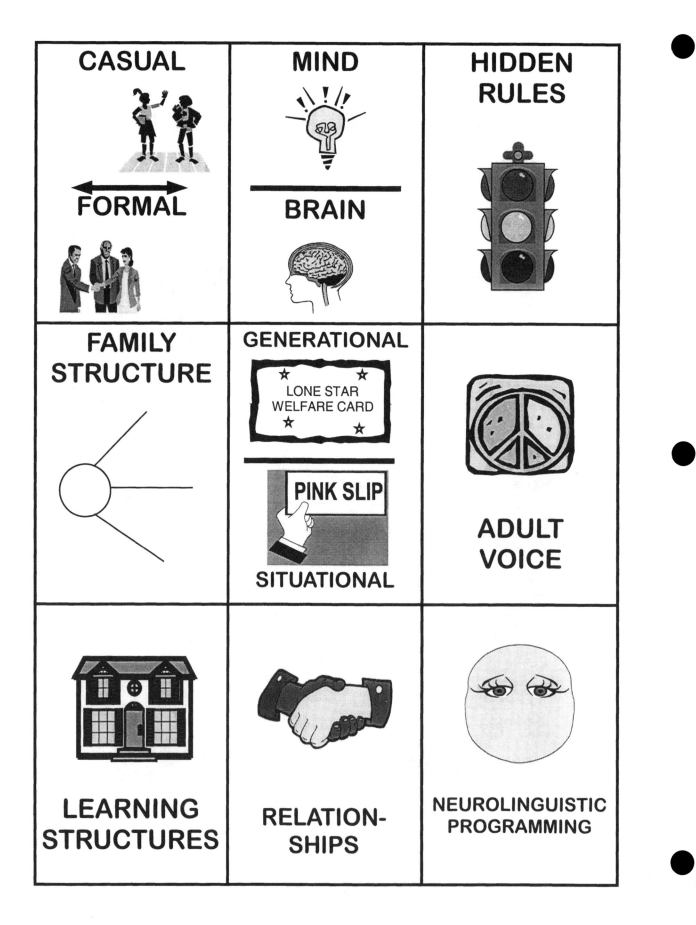

CASUAL ⟷ FORMAL	**MIND / BRAIN**	**HIDDEN RULES**
FAMILY STRUCTURE	**GENERATIONAL** LONE STAR WELFARE CARD / PINK SLIP **SITUATIONAL**	**ADULT VOICE**
LEARNING STRUCTURES	**RELATION-SHIPS**	**NEUROLINGUISTIC PROGRAMMING**

U.S. MEDIAN INCOME FOR PERSONS AGE 25 AND OLDER, BY SEX AND EDUCATIONAL ATTAINMENT: 2001

	Overall	Less than Ninth grade	Grades 9-12 (no diploma)	HS Diploma (includes GED)	Associate Degree	Bachelor's Degree	Master's Degree	Professional Degree	Doctorate
				Numbers of persons with income (in thousands)					
Male	84,389	5,809	7,421	25,954	6,352	15,723	5,522	1,749	1,488
Female	88,075	5,196	7,376	28,945	8,177	15,660	5,749	899	653
				Median income, in 2001 dollars					
Male	$32,494	$14,594	$19,434	$28,343	$38,870	$54,069	$61,960	$81,602	$72,642
Female	$18,549	$ 8,846	$10,330	$15,665	$22,638	$30,973	$40,744	$46,635	$52,181

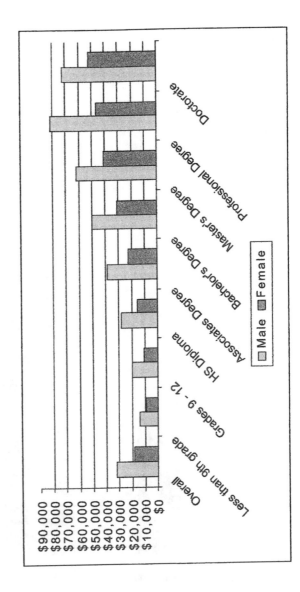

Source: U.S. Bureau of the Census

POVERTY STATISTICS

Extreme poverty, poverty, and near-poverty rates for children under age 6 by living arrangement, 2001.

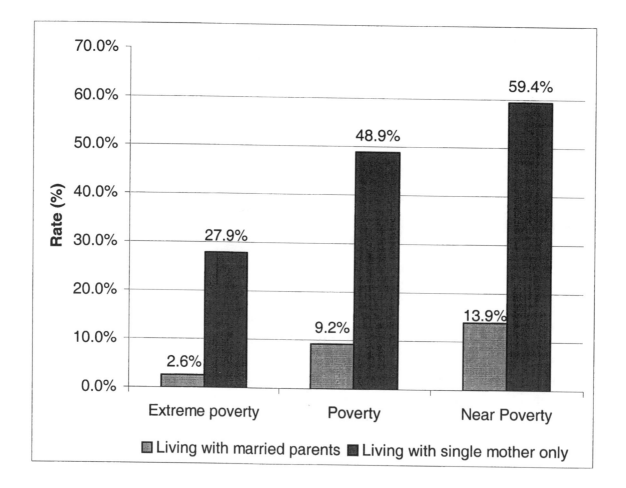

Source: U.S. Bureau of the Census

MODULE TWO

RESOURCES

RESOURCES

FINANCIAL	HAVING THE MONEY TO PURCHASE GOODS AND SERVICES.
EMOTIONAL	BEING ABLE TO CHOOSE AND CONTROL EMOTIONAL RESPONSES, PARTICULARLY TO NEGATIVE SITUATIONS, WITHOUT ENGAGING IN SELF-DESTRUCTIVE BEHAVIOR. THIS IS AN INTERNAL RESOURCE AND SHOWS ITSELF THROUGH STAMINA, PERSERVERANCE, AND CHOICES.
MENTAL	HAVING THE MENTAL ABILITIES AND ACQUIRED SKILLS (READING, WRITING, COMPUTING) TO DEAL WITH DAILY LIFE.
SPIRITUAL	BELIEVING IN DIVINE PURPOSE AND GUIDANCE.
PHYSICAL	HAVING PHYSICAL HEALTH AND MOBILITY.
SUPPORT SYSTEMS	HAVING FRIENDS, FAMILY, AND BACKUP RESOURCES AVAILABLE TO ACCESS IN TIMES OF NEED. THESE ARE EXTERNAL RESOURCES.
RELATIONSHIPS/ROLE MODELS	HAVING FREQUENT ACCESS TO ADULT(S) WHO ARE APPROPRIATE, WHO ARE NURTURING TO THE CHILD, AND WHO DO NOT ENGAGE IN SELF-DESTRUCTIVE BEHAVIOR.
KNOWLEDGE OF HIDDEN RULES	KNOWING THE UNSPOKEN CUES AND HABITS OF A GROUP.

RESOURCE ANALYSIS

NAME	FINANCIAL RESOURCES	EMOTIONAL RESOURCES	MENTAL RESOURCES	SPIRITUAL RESOURCES	PHYSICAL RESOURCES	SUPPORT SYSTEMS	ROLE MODELS	KNOWLEDGE OF HIDDEN RULES

aha! Process, Inc. • (800) 424-9484

SALLY AND SUEANN

BACKGROUND

Sally is an 8-year-old white girl whose mother, SueAnn, has been married and divorced twice. Her mother works two jobs and does not receive child support. An older sister is pregnant. Sally has two stepsiblings – one younger and one older. The current stepfather's favorite child is the youngest child, a son. The stepfather is laid off right now.

You are Sally's mother, SueAnn, a 33-year-old white female. You are on your third marriage. You have four children by four different men. You are working two jobs right now because your current husband has been laid off. He is supposed to be taking care of the kids, but he doesn't like to be tied down. You got pregnant when you were a senior in high school, so you were unable to finish school. You knew who the father was, but he changed his mind and wouldn't marry you. You kept the child, and she is now 15 and pregnant. Your second child is Sally, and she is 8 years old. Between the two jobs, you bring home about $400 a week, and you are exhausted. You make the girls cook and clean. You are very tired. Lately you and your husband have been fighting a lot. Your mother and father are divorced and live in the same town that you do. You remember how much you loved to dance country-western and party. All you wish for now is sleep. You may have to move again soon because you're so far behind on the bills.

CURRENT SITUATION

You get a call at work. You had let your husband drop you off at work because he was going to fix the muffler. Your husband is now in jail. He was caught driving while intoxicated. This is the second time he has been caught. You need $500 to pay the bondsman to get him out of jail. Furthermore, he was driving your car, which didn't have insurance. They have towed the car, and the towing bill is $80. Each day it's impounded it will cost you $40 in parking fees, and you can't get the car out until you have proof of insurance. When and if your husband gets out of jail, he will need to see the probation officer, which will cost him $60 each visit.

Your pregnant daughter needs $400 to pay the doctor so that he will keep seeing her. You have told her she needs to go to the clinic where the service is free. However, the wait is usually three to four hours, and she misses a half day of school. There is also the problem of getting her there. It's in a bad part of town, and it will be dark before you can get there to pick her up.

The bill collector calls you at work and tells you he is going to take you to court for overdue electric bills at the last place you lived. You now live in an apartment where the utilities are paid, but you are behind on your rent by a month. You were OK until your husband got laid off. You are out of birth-control pills. To refill the prescription, you have to go to the clinic and wait three to four hours, and you can't take that much time off work. Also, you need $20 for the birth-control pills. Lately your husband has been looking at Sally in ways that you don't like. But you are so tired.

What are Sally and SueAnn's resources? On p. 9 put a check under the resources that are present, a minus under the ones that are not and a question mark where the resources are uncertain.

 aha! Process, Inc. • (800) 424-9484

OTIS AND VANGIE

BACKGROUND

Otis is a 9-year-old black boy. His mother conceived him at 14, dropped out of school, and is on welfare. Otis has two younger siblings and one older sibling who is a gang member.

You are Otis's mother, Vangie. You are a 23-year-old black female. You were the oldest of five children. You had your first child when you were 15. You have received welfare and food stamps since the birth of your first child. You lived with your mother until your fourth child was born when you were 18. Then you got your own place. You dropped out of school when you were pregnant with Otis. School was always difficult for you, and you never did feel comfortable reading much anyway. Your current boyfriend comes often and he works sometimes. Your mother lives down the street. Your weekly income (including food stamps) is $215. You move a lot because there are always more bills at the end of the month than money.

CURRENT SITUATION

Your sister calls and tells you that her boyfriend has beaten her again, and she needs to come spend the night at your house. The last time she came she stayed for two weeks, and her 12-year-old handicapped son would not leave your 5-year-old daughter alone. You have several choices: (1) You could take her in and make her pay for her meals, (2) you could not take her in and have the whole family mad at you, (3) you could tell your daughter to hit her cousin when he comes close, (4) you could make Otis take care of the handicapped son, (5) you could slap the fool out of the handicapped son, (6) you could use the rent money to pay for the extra food, (7) you could go partying together and let Otis take care of the kids, or (8) you could move to a bigger place.

Otis comes home from school and announces that the school is going to have a reading contest. For every five books you read to him, he will receive a coupon to get $2 off a pizza. To obtain his books, he needs you to go to the library. Also, you aren't sure you can even read to him because your skills were never good, and you haven't read for a long time. Getting to the library requires that you walk because you don't have a car. There have been two drive-by shootings last week. He also tells you that the school is having an open house and is sending a bus around the neighborhood to pick up parents. He gives you a note that you can't read.

You are probably going to have to move again. This week Otis got cut badly at school, and the school nurse took him to the emergency room; they want $200. Rent is due for the month, and it's $300 for three bedrooms. Sister is coming, and that means extra food because she never has any money. Your boyfriend got arrested and wants you to get him out of jail. He was arrested for assault. The bondsman wants $500. Your ex-boyfriend knew better than to come around. You need your boyfriend because his money makes it possible to keep from going hungry.

The teacher calls and tells you that Otis is misbehaving again. You beat the fool out of him with a belt and tell him he better behave. But that night you fix him his favorite dinner, then you tell everyone you talk to how Otis is misbehaving and what a burden he is to you.

What are Otis and Vangie's resources? On p. 9 put a check under the resources that are present, a minus under the ones that are not and a question mark where the resources are uncertain.

aha! Process, Inc. • (800) 424-9484

JOHN AND ADELE

BACKGROUND

John is an 8-year-old white boy. His father is a doctor and remarried but does not see his children. He pays minimal child support. The mother, Adele, works part time and is an alcoholic. One younger sibling, a girl who is mentally and physically handicapped, lives with the mother and John.

You are Adele, John's mother. You are a 29-year-old white female. You quit college your sophomore year so that you could go to work to support John's father as he went through medical school. You were both elated when John was born. During the time your husband was an intern, you found that a drink or two or three in the evening calmed you down, especially since your husband was gone so much. When your second child was born, she was severely handicapped. Both of you were in shock. A year later your husband finished his residency, announced that he was in love with another woman, and divorced you. Last you heard, your husband is driving a Porsche, and he and his new wife spent their most recent vacation in Cancún. Your parents are dead. You have a sister who lives 50 miles away. Your weekly income, including child support, is $300 before taxes. Your handicapped child is 3 years old and is in day care provided by the school district.

CURRENT SITUATION

You have been late to work for the third time this month. Your car broke down, and it will take $400 to fix it. Your boss told you that you will be docked a day's pay – and that if you're late again, you will be fired. You don't know how you're going to get to work tomorrow. You consider several choices: (1) You can go car shopping, (2) you can put the car in the garage and worry about the money later, (3) you can invite the mechanic over for dinner, (4) you can get mad and quit, (5) you can call your ex and threaten to take him back to court unless he pays for the car, (6) you can get a second job, or (7) you can get drunk.

Your daughter has had another seizure, and you took her to the doctor (one of the reasons you were late for work). The new medicine will cost you $45 every month.

John comes home from school and announces that the school is going to have a reading contest. Every book you read with him will earn points for him. Each book is one point, and he wants to earn 100 points. You must do physical therapy with your daughter each evening for 30 minutes, as well as get dinner. For John to get his books, he needs you to go to the library with him. You have only enough gas to go to work and back for the rest of the week, maybe not that. He also tells you that the school is having an open house, and he will get a pencil if you come. But John is not old enough to watch your daughter. Your ex has already threatened to bring up in court that you are an unfit mother if you try to get more money from him.

The mechanic calls and invites you out to dinner. He tells you that you might be able to work something out in terms of payment. It has been a long time since you have been out, and he is good-looking and seems like a nice man.

What are Adele and John's resources? On p. 9 put a check under the resources that are present, a minus under the ones that are not and a question mark where the resources are uncertain.

aha! Process, Inc. • (800) 424-9484

OPIE AND OPRAH

BACKGROUND

Opie is a 12-year-old African-American girl and the oldest of five children. She runs the household because her mother, Oprah, works long hours as a domestic. Grandmother, who is 80, is senile and lives with them, as well as an out-of-work uncle.

You are Opie's mother, Oprah. You are a 32-year-old black female. You were married for 10 years to your husband, and then he was killed in a car accident on the way to work two years ago. You work long hours as a domestic for a doctor. You go to the Missionary Baptist Church every Sunday where you lead the choir. Your employer treats you well and you take home about $300 every week. You ride public transportation to work and the church bus on Sunday. You want your children to go to college, even though you only finished high school.

CURRENT SITUATION

Your employer gives you a $400 Christmas bonus. You thank the Lord at church for the gift. After church, three different people approach you privately. One asks for $50 to have the electricity turned on; one asks for $100 to feed her brother's family; one asks for $60 to replace a pair of broken glasses. You were hoping to save some money for an emergency.

Opie has the opportunity to be in a state-sponsored competition that requires after-school practices. You want her to do that, but you must have her at home after school every day.

What resources do Opie and Oprah have? On p. 9 put a check under the resources that are present, a minus under the ones that are not and a question mark where the resources are uncertain.

EILEEN AND WISTERIA

BACKGROUND

Eileen is a 10-year-old white girl who lives with her 70-year-old grandmother, Wisteria, who is on Social Security. Eileen doesn't know who her father is. Her mother has been arrested four times for prostitution and/or drug possession in the last two years. About once a year, Mother sobers up for a month and wants Eileen back as her child.

You are Eileen's grandmother, Wisteria. You get about $150 a week from Social Security. Your daughter, Eileen's mother, has been in trouble for years. You have given up on her, and you couldn't stand to see Eileen in a foster home, so you have taken her into your home. Eileen's mother was never sure who the father was; she is a drug addict and has been arrested frequently. One of her various pimps or boyfriends usually gets her out of jail. Once a year, when she sobers up for a short period of time, she gives Eileen lots of attention and then leaves. The last time she came and left, Eileen cried and cried and said she never wanted to see her mother again. You have a little money in savings, but you don't want to use it yet. Your house is paid for, and you have a decent car. You worry what will happen to Eileen if you get sick or die, and you pray each day to live until Eileen is 18. You don't see as well as you once did. All your relatives are either dead or distant. Every Sunday you and Eileen go to the United Methodist Church where you have been a member for 40 years.

CURRENT SITUATION

Eileen comes home from school with an assigned project. She must do a family history and interview as many relatives as possible. You aren't sure what to say to Eileen.

The teacher tells you at a conference that Eileen has an imaginary friend whom she talks to a great deal during the day. The teacher recommends that you seek counseling for Eileen. She knows a counselor who would charge only $40 a session. She also comments that Eileen's clothes are old-fashioned and that she doesn't fit in very well with the other students. You don't tell the teacher that you make Eileen's clothes. The teacher suggests that you let Eileen have friends over so she can socialize, but you don't know if anyone would come – or if you could stand the noise.

What are Eileen and Wisteria's resources? On p. 9 put a check under the resources that are present, a minus under the ones that are not and a question mark where the resources are uncertain.

aha! Process, Inc. • (800) 424-9484

JUAN AND RAMÓN

BACKGROUND

Juan is a 6-year-old Hispanic boy who lives with his uncle Ramón. Juan's father was killed in a gang-related killing. His uncle is angry about the death of Juan's father. When his uncle is not around, Juan stays with his grandmother, who speaks no English. The uncle makes his living selling drugs but is very respectful toward his mother.

You are Juan's uncle, Ramón, a 25-year-old Hispanic male. You doubt that you will live many more years because you know that most of the people like you are either dead or in jail. You are angry. Your brother, Juan's father, was killed by a rival gang two years ago when Juan was 4. Juan is your godchild, and you will defend him with your blood. Juan's mother was a piece of white trash and wouldn't take care of Juan like a good mother should. She is in jail now for gang-related activities. You leave Juan with your mother often because the activities you're involved in are too dangerous to have Juan along. You are a leader in your gang and sell drugs as well. Your mother speaks only Spanish, but you have taught Juan to be very respectful toward her. She goes to Mass every Sunday and takes Juan with her when she can. You make $1,000 a week on the average.

CURRENT SITUATION

Juan comes home with a notice about a parent-teacher conference. You are away, hiding from the police. Grandmother cannot read Spanish or English.

The rival gang has killed another one of your gang members. This has forced you to be away from Juan more than you would like. Plans are that you will kill the leader of the rival gang, but then you will need to go to Mexico for some time to hide. You are thinking about taking Juan with you because he is all in the world that you love. You are stockpiling money. You don't want to take him out of school, but he is only 6; he can catch up. You don't think you'll live past 30, and you want to have time with him.

What resources do Juan and Ramón have? On p. 9 put a check under the resources that are present, a minus under the ones that are not and a question mark where the resources are uncertain.

MARIA AND NOEMI

BACKGROUND

Maria is a 10-year-old Hispanic girl. Her mother does not drive or speak English. Father speaks some English. Maria is a second-generation Hispanic born in the United States. Mother does not work outside the home. Father works for minimum wage as a concrete worker. There are five children. The family gets food stamps, and the mother is a devout Catholic.

You are Maria's mother, Noemi. You are a 27-year-old Hispanic female. You have five children. You have been married to your husband for 11 years and you love him and your children very much. Children always come first. As a child, you and your parents were migrant workers, so you are happy that you have a place to live and do not need to move around. Because of the migrant work, you didn't go past the sixth grade. Your husband works on a construction crew laying concrete. When it's not raining and when there's plenty of building, he has lots of work. Sometimes, though, he will go two or three weeks with no work and, therefore, no money. Your parents live in your town, and they try to help you when times are bad. You get food stamps to help out. You go to Mass every Sunday, and often on weekends you go to your parents' place with your children and brothers and sisters. Your husband is a good man, and he loves his children. On a good week he will bring home $400.

CURRENT SITUATION

Maria comes home and says she has to do a salt map. You have just spent all the money for the week on food – and she needs five pounds of flour, two pounds of salt, and a piece of board to put it on. She also needs to get information from an encyclopedia, whatever that is. The car has broken down and will require $100 for parts. The baby is sick, and medicine will be $30. It has rained for two weeks, and your husband hasn't had any work or pay.

The teacher has asked Maria to stay after school and be in an academic contest. You expect her to get married and have children just as you have. But for now you need her to help you with the children.

What resources do Maria and Noemi have? On p. 9 put a check under the resources that are present, a minus under the ones that are not and a question mark where the resources are uncertain.

aha! Process, Inc. • (800) 424-9484

TIJUANA CHECOSOVAKIA

BACKGROUND

You are a 14-year-old African American female. Your mother named you Tijuana Checosovakia because she heard that on television and liked the name. You had your first child at 9 years of age and your second one at 13 years of age. You are now a freshman in high school.

You live in a rural area and go to the local high school. There are several state schools for juvenile delinquents in the area, and you like to hang around the fences and look at the boys.

CURRENT SITUATION

Last month your mother found out that she was pregnant. Your 15-year-old sister is pregnant also. You are sure glad you aren't pregnant right now because they are so moody.

You are in a family literacy program as a part of the requirement for receiving state aid. Last week you and the other teenage mothers in this program were to go to an amusement park with the babies as a way of learning to engage in family activities. But neither you nor the other girls are fools. You left your babies at home and wore your tightest clothes. Those teachers made you go back home, change clothes, and bring the babies. So stupid!!

Last week was the first day you were back in school again. You come to school because it is a part of this family literacy requirement. The principal made you take out your nose ring. You demanded that she find you a broomstraw so that you could put it in your nose to keep that hole open. You paid good money for that nose piercing. And then that principal is so dumb. She told you that you would look funny with the broomstick sticking out of your nose. She didn't even know that you just burn the end off and it keeps the hole open. You wonder how that principal stays alive.

And then the counselor wants to know why you got pregnant and why the fathers were listed as unknown. You told the counselor that you didn't want the babies' fathers involved. Those are your babies – only yours.

What are Tijuana Checosovakia's resources? On p. 9 put a check under the resources that are present, a minus under the ones that are not and a question mark where the resources are uncertain.

HABIB

BACKGROUND

You are a African American male, age 18. The reason you come to school is that it is a condition of your probation. You are not really a bad person. It just seems that you are always at the wrong place at the wrong time. You don't have a malicious bone in your body; you are likable and easily persuaded. Your one great attribute is that you are one heck of a fighter. The women like you. You played on the football team, but you just couldn't keep up the grades. And besides, women were much more fun than football.

You went on probation when you were 16. You and the boys were looking for something to do, so you broke into the local pawnshop. It was one of those days that just was no good. You had come home from school and found your mama beaten up by her latest boyfriend. Shirley, your younger sister, had taken her two babies and left. You called an ambulance for your mother, but you didn't go to the hospital. She will miss a couple days of work because of the beating. You would like to help with the money, but you can't get a job because of your arrest and the fact that you are on probation for armed robbery.

So you were mad when you went looking for the boyfriend. Your girlfriend was mad at you; so breaking into the pawn shop sounded like a good idea at the time. But you got caught and were charged with armed robbery. Juan had loaned you his gun and you had put it into your pocket.

CURRENT SITUATION

You are in alternative school. You can read fairly well. You like people and enjoy being with them. But in your heart you are scared for your younger brother. As you wrote to the teacher one day, "I want my little brother to be successful in life. I want him to be the best he can be in whatever he want to do. But I know I don't want him to hang in the streets, 'cause the streets are not going to lead a good life for him. I know from experience 'cause I rapped up in the streets, and it ain't cool. All the cool ones dead. It's all based on money. Money run the system so I'm gonna make sure I have plenty of that."

What are Habib's resources? On p. 9 put a check under the resources that are present, a minus under the ones that are not and a question mark where the resources are uncertain.

aha! Process, Inc. • (800) 424-9484

GERALDO

BACKGROUND

You are a Hispanic male, 13 years old, and you are in seventh grade. You are a prominent gang member. It's a matter of pride. When you were 11, you watched your 18-year-old cousin put a gun in his mouth and shoot himself. Your other cousin, who was 17 at the time, ran out of the room and killed himself by running his car under an 18-wheeler.

Your mother attends mass every Saturday, and you love her. You know the rules of the house. However, the street is different. Last week, your gang made $4,000 selling drugs. This money was split among 10 members.

CURRENT SITUATION

Today is the anniversary of your cousins' deaths. You took a little acid before you went to school today. It seemed like the only way to face school. You really like your reading teacher, but all you could do was giggle. It sure beats crying. You haven't turned in your assignments for the last two weeks, but then again, you could do almost all the assignments with one hand tied behind your back if you felt like it.

You are watching your back. Today one of the policemen was at school doing an assembly on drugs. He watched you, and you watched him. Rumor has it that there will be a fight between your gang and another rival gang soon.

But today in particular you watched Tony at lunch. Tony's dad drives a Mercedes and drops him off every morning at school. You wonder what it must be like to have money and not worry about dying. There is no reason to do well in school; you know you're going to be dead before you're 25. You might as well enjoy life and girls. As you wrote to your teacher, "I would like adults to know that people my age are different than when they came up. They grew up different than I did. I grew up with sex, money, and murder and banging in the streets, and that's not all. They expect me to do what they want. Well, what they want at home is easy, but as soon as I leave those four walls of home sweet home comes the hard life. As soon as I'm in the streets, it turns into a nightmare, not like my house. It makes me want to die and get away from the violence. I guess that's why I have no one, because faithful is not in my vocabulary. I'm only faithful to them streets."

What are Geraldo's resources? On p. 9 put a check under the resources that are present, a minus under the ones that are not and a question mark where the resources are uncertain.

    aha! Process, Inc. • (800) 424-9484

STEVE

BACKGROUND

You are a 17-year-old white male, a senior in high school. For as long as you can remember, your father has been a mean drunk. But you haven't been home since you were 14, when he kicked you out. Your mother cried and cried, but then he beat her into silence.

You remember the night you were kicked out. You had no place to go, so you slept on the church steps because you believed you would be safe there. You rummaged food from the garbage bins of the fast-food places and restaurants. You kept on going to school because at least you were safe there. You got a job at a restaurant, even though you were underage, and you got a cheap apartment after a couple of months.

CURRENT SITUATION

At 16 you got a full-time job working in the evenings for minimum wage. There's a counselor at school who keeps track of you and how you're doing in school. This week he came with a stack of homework that you need to do in math. Your brother is living with you now as well. You have told the counselor that you think you will just quit. You are so discouraged, and the math teacher told you in front of the class yesterday that anyone who was a senior and still in Algebra I might as well drop out of school.

But the counselor told you he was counting on you. He knew it was rough, but he knew you could do it. So you agreed to do the homework for the counselor. God knows you hate the algebra teacher. The counselor told you to come by at 7 in the morning and he would help you with the algebra.

There are no girls in your life. All you have time to do is go to work, go to school, and sleep.

What are Steve's resources? On p. 9 put a check under the resources that are present, a minus under the ones that are not and a question mark where the resources are uncertain.

MAGNOLIA

BACKGROUND

You are in the 10th grade and are a white female, 16 years old. You barely made it to school today on time because you had to get your eight brothers and sisters ready for school. Your mother didn't come home last night and you aren't sure where she is. You just hope and pray you get to the mailbox before she does when the welfare check comes in. Two weeks ago you called in sick so that you could wait and get the mail. Then you lied to your mother and said that the check hadn't come. But there was no food in the house, and you couldn't let your brothers and sisters starve.

Your grades are B's and C's and you feel happy about that. You could get straight A's if you had time to do your projects. You ace most of the tests, but you don't have time to do the homework. One of the teachers last week told you that you were bright but lazy. You didn't say anything. How could you begin to explain? The only things that are constant in your life are your brothers and sisters, who have five different fathers.

You can't remember a time that you didn't take care of them. You remember when you used to steal from the people you baby-sat for because your mother told you to do that. But it just made you feel dirty, so you refused to steal, even when that meant you had to go hungry. You can't remember a time when you haven't been hungry sometime during a week.

You want to be a teacher. You remember your fifth-grade teacher who brought you a turkey and meal on Thanksgiving. You were so grateful because there had been no food. You believe that if you were a teacher you could help kids also.

CURRENT SITUATION

The teacher is lecturing on the civilization of Greece, and you are interested, but you are wondering what is happening at home. You left your 4-year-old brother alone because you couldn't miss any more school this six weeks, and your mother still wasn't home. But he has stayed at home alone before.

Last night Sally cried because she didn't have three dollars to go on the field trip. Johnny cried because he couldn't go to a birthday party. You don't have a car. The girls in P.E. today laughed at you because you are fat, but you know that fat might keep you alive. You have to eat when it's there. Besides, you have no desire to be attractive to men. You know what it can do. The girls right now are passing notes about their dates. You just want to make sure your 4-year-old brother is OK.

What are Magnolia's resources? On p. 9 put a check under the resources that are present, a minus under the ones that are not and a question mark where the resources are uncertain.

25 aha! Process, Inc. • (800) 424-9484

TAHITI AND THERESA

BACKGROUND

You are Tahiti, age 14. Your father was an African American, and your mother was from Mexico. Theresa is your best friend. She is also 14. Her mother was from Mexico, and her father was from Puerto Rico. You each want to have a baby. School has never been easy for you or for Theresa. So all you talk about are boys.

Theresa has been luckier than you have been. Both of you have been trying since you were 13 to get pregnant. Both of you are very pretty, and you each have a boyfriend. But Theresa is luckier than you. She and her boyfriend, Miguel, have been having sex at least twice a week for a month now. Miguel is a member of the toughest gang on the streets, and he is a real homeboy. But your boyfriend, Raul, only wants to make love after he has been drinking, and then he's rough.

Lately one of the rival gang members, Gilberto, is looking at you and has touched you in the hall when Raul wasn't looking. But you know Raul and the gang would hurt him. You want a baby so much.

CURRENT SITUATION

Today in class the teacher moved Gilberto so that he now sits next to you. He wrote you a note asking to meet you after school at a certain place. You tell him yes because you want to make love. You want a baby, and you want Raul to know that he can't be messing around all the time with your love. Besides, it has been boring lately.

Your father works at the refinery and brings home about $600 a week. Your mother stays at home. But last night they had a knock-down fight; he had been drinking. You left the house for a while.

You are failing in school. School really doesn't matter because you're going to have a baby and stay at home just like your mother did. There is no other way. Meanwhile, you hope you can get pregnant before Theresa does. Then you will have something of your own.

What are Tahiti's resources? On p. 9 put a check under the resources that are present, a minus under the ones that are not and a question mark where the resources are uncertain.

RAQUEL

BACKGROUND

You are Raquel, a 15-year-old white female. You are about 5'6" and 140 pounds. You are intelligent and cynical and could pass for a 20-year-old. You have been on your own for a long time. Right now you are in alternative school. You just can't handle regular high school.

When you were 11, your father and mother divorced. Your parents made more than $100,000 a year before the divorce, but even then they both did drugs – cocaine, designer drugs, etc. Then when you were 11, the divorce occurred and you and your sister, who was 4 at the time, went with your father as a part of the custody settlement. He moved with you to a city several hundred miles away. His drug habit caught up with him, and he drank alcohol daily. In fact, he was drunk most of the time. His only job was selling cocaine and marijuana, and he couldn't even keep up with that. You knew that, if you didn't do something, you and your sister would starve. So you went to school every day so that you weren't taken away from your father – you didn't want to go back to your mother – but at night you made the sales he couldn't make during the day. At age twelve you bought a car on your own and drove so that you could make the deliveries. You made sure your sister was taken care of and got to kindergarten. You didn't tell anyone. But some days you didn't learn much at school because you were so tired. It was a good thing school wasn't hard for you.

Your father was arrested when you were 14, and you went to live with relatives. You returned to regular high school, but one day one of the students made a comment about your father being in jail. You were so angry you couldn't see straight. But then you heard one of the high school boys talking about your 8-year-old sister and how she would make a good lay, and you beat the _____ out of him. You knew how many men you had to fight off yourself during the drug days. That's how you got into alternative school. All you really love is your sister, and you intend to make sure she doesn't live through your hell.

aha! Process, Inc. • (800) 424-9484

CURRENT SITUATION

You live with your grandmother (your father's mother). She didn't particularly want you, but your father made her promise. There is not much money, and you can't legally drive yet, even though you know how. Yesterday, when you got home, Grandmother was watching the soap operas and the house was a pigsty. A clean house is really important to you, and you kept yours clean when you were in charge. You can't say anything because Grandmother gets angry. So you cleaned it up. Someone was in your room also, going through your things. But you can't say anything. One of her sons is living there right now because his wife kicked him out; you keep an eagle eye on your sister.

Today at school one of the teachers took 40 points away from you because you told Todd, the dumb 19-year-old who sits next to you, to _____ off because he wanted to know if you would be "available" for $20. It seems like the teacher doesn't have a clue about what the homeboys mean when they're talking or what goes on in her class. Sylvia, the 18-year-old in your class who is a stripper, thinks she might be pregnant and asks you what to do. You look in her eyes and see your own reflection and wonder how you ever got mixed up with this group. You are so lonely and wonder if this is all life has to offer and what you ever did to deserve this. You remember better times but know you'll have to go to college to get out of this situation. But you wonder how long you can stand all the stupid people around you. You can't commit suicide because you love your younger sister, and you must be there for her. You're counting the days until you're 18, because then you'll be free.

What are Raquel's resources? On p. 9 put a check under the resources that are present, a minus under the ones that are not and a question mark where the resources are uncertain.

MODULE THREE

LANGUAGE, STORY STRUCTURE, COGNITION

REGISTERS OF LANGUAGE

REGISTER	EXPLANATION
FROZEN	Language that is always the same. For example: Lord's Prayer, wedding vows, etc.
FORMAL	The standard sentence syntax and word choice of work and school. Has complete sentences and specific word choice.
CONSULTATIVE	Formal register when used in conversation. Discourse pattern not quite as direct as formal register.
CASUAL	Language between friends and is characterized by a 400- to 800-word vocabulary. Word choice general and not specific. Conversation dependent upon non-verbal assists. Sentence syntax often incomplete.
INTIMATE	Language between lovers or twins. Language of sexual harrassment.

Cognitive Strategies*

INPUT:
quantity and quality of data gathered

1. Use planning behaviors.
2. Focus perception on specific stimulus.
3. Control impulsivity.
4. Explore data systematically.
5. Use appropriate and accurate labels.
6. Organize space using stable systems of reference.
7. Orient data in time.
8. Identify constancies across variations.
9. Gather precise and accurate data.
10. Consider two sources of information at once.
11. Organize data (parts of a whole).
12. Visually transport data.

1. Identify and define the problem.
2. Select relevant cues.
3. Compare data.
4. Select appropriate categories of time.
5. Summarize data.
6. Project relationships of data.
7. Use logical data.
8. Test hypothesis.
9. Build inferences.
10. Make a plan using the data.
11. Use appropriate labels.
12. Use data systematically.

ELABORATION:
efficient use of the data

OUTPUT:
communication of elaboration and input

1. Communicate clearly the labels and process.
2. Visually transport data correctly.
3. Use precise and accurate language.
4. Control impulsive behavior.

*adapted from the work of Reuven Feuerstein

aha! Process, Inc. • (800) 424-9484

IF AN INDIVIDUAL DEPENDS UPON A RANDOM, EPISODIC STORY STRUCTURE FOR MEMORY PATTERNS, LIVES IN AN UNPREDICTABLE ENVIRONMENT, **AND HAS NOT DEVELOPED THE ABILITY TO PLAN,** THEN ...

IF AN INDIVIDUAL CANNOT PLAN, HE/SHE **CANNOT PREDICT.**

IF AN INDIVIDUAL CANNOT PREDICT, HE/SHE **CANNOT IDENTIFY CAUSE AND EFFECT.**

IF AN INDIVIDUAL CANNOT IDENTIFY CAUSE AND EFFECT, HE/SHE **CANNOT IDENTIFY CONSEQUENCE.**

IF AN INDIVIDUAL CANNOT IDENTIFY CONSEQUENCE, HE/SHE **CANNOT CONTROL IMPULSIVITY.**

IF AN INDIVIDUAL CANNOT CONTROL IMPULSIVITY, HE/SHE _____.

	MEDIATION	
Identification of the stimulus	Assignment of meaning	Identification of a strategy

aha! Process, Inc. • (800) 424-9484

MODULE FOUR

FAMILY STRUCTURE

CASE STUDY (Bold type indicates the narrator; plain type indicates comments from various listeners. Names have been changed to protect the girl.)

WALTER (white male)

As the story would be told in poverty ... probably by a relative or neighbor:

Well, you know Walter got put away for 37 years. Him being 48 and all. He'll probably die in jail. Just couldn't leave his hands off that 12-year-old Susie. Dirty old man. Bodding's gonna whup his tail. **Already did. You know Bodding was waiting for him in jail and beat the living daylights out of him.** In jail? **Yeah, Bodding got caught for possession. Had $12,000 on him when they arrested him.** Golly, wish I had been there to cash in!!!! (laughter) A man's gotta make a living! **Susie being blind and all – I can see why Bodding beat the daylights out of Walter. Lucky he didn't get killed, old Walter is.** Too bad her momma is no good. **She started the whole thing! Susie's momma goes over there and argues with Bodding.** Ain't they divorced? **Yeah, and she's got Walter working for her, repairing her house or something.** Or something, I bet. What's she got in her house that's worth fixing? **Anyway, she goes over to Bodding's house to take the lawnmower ...** I reckon so as Walter can mow the yard?? I bet that's the first time old Walter has ever broken a sweat! Reminds me of the time I saw Walter thinking about taking a job. All that thinking and he had to get drunk. He went to jail that time, too – a felony, I think it was. So many of those DWIs. Judge told him he was egregious. Walter said he wasn't greasy – he took a bath last week!!! (laughter) **Bodding and Susie's momma got in a fight, so she tells Walter to take Susie with him.** Lordy, her elevator must not go all the way to the top!! Didn't she know about him getting arrested for enticing a minor??? **With Susie blind and all. And she sends Susie with Walter?** She sure don't care about her babies. **Well, Walter's momma was there 'cause Walter lives with his momma, seeing as how he can't keep no job.** Ain't his other brother there? **Yeah, and him 41 years old. That poor momma sure has her burdens to bear. And then her 30-year-old daughter, Susie's momma, at home, too. You know Susie's momma lost custody of her kids. Walter gets these videos, you know. Those adult videos. Heavy breathing!** (laughter) Some of them are more fun to listen to than look at! (laughter) Those people in the

aha! Process, Inc. • (800) 424-9484

videos are des-per-ate!! **Anyway, he puts those on and then carries Susie to his room and tells her she wants him – and describes all his sex-u-al exploits!!** Golly, he must be a loooooooooover. (laughter) He should be shot. I'd kill him if he did that to my kid!! **Then he lets his fingers do the walking**. Kinda like the Yellow Pages! (laughter) **I guess he didn't do anything with his "thang," according to Miss Rosie who went to that trial every day. And Susie begging him to stop so many times.** Probably couldn't do anything with it; that's why he needs to listen to that heavy breathing! Pant! Pant! (laughter) What a no-count, low-down creep. I'll pay Bodding to kill him!! **Bodding says the only way Walter is coming out of jail is in a pine box.** Don't blame him myself. **Yeah, Miss Rosie said Walter's momma said at the trial that the door to Walter's room was open and there ain't no way Walter could have done that. That she is a good Christian momma and she don't put up with that.** Oh Lordy, did God strike her dead on the spot, or is she still alive??? I'd be afraid of ending up in eternal damnation for telling a story like that! **Miss Rosie said her 12-year-old nephew testified that the door was closed and his grandma told him to say it was open!!!!** Ooo! Ooo! Oooo! That poor baby tells the truth? His grandma's gonna make him mis-er-a-ble!!! **And then Walter's momma tells that jury that she never allows those adult videos in her house, leastways not that she pays for them!!** (lots of laughter) I bet the judge bit on that one!! How is Walter gonna get videos except for her money? Mowing yards? (more laughter) No, I bet he saves his pennies!! (laughter) **All these years she has covered for Walter. Guess she just couldn't cover no more.** Remember that time Walter got drunk and wrecked her car, and she said she was driving? And she was at the hospital at the time with a broken leg. And the judge asked her how she could be driving and in the hospital "simultaneously." And she said that's just how it was – simultaneously – she had never felt so excited in her life. (laughter) Who turned Walter in? **Well, it wasn't Susie's momma. She was busy with Skeeter, her new boyfriend. I hear he's something.** Remember that one boyfriend she had? Thought he was so smart? **Speaking of smart, that Susie sure is. Her blind and all, and she won the district spelling bee for the seventh grade this year. I hear she's in National Honor Society, whatever that is.** Wonder if it's kinda like the country club. Instead of playing golf, you just spell!!! (laughter) **Susie calls this friend of hers who tells her mother and they come and get her and take her to the police and hospital.** Some rich lady, not minding her own business, that's for sure. **Well, it was a good thing for Susie, 'cause that momma of hers sure ain't good for Susie. She don't deserve a kid like Susie. SHE oughta be the one who's blind**. Ain't that the truth. Way I see it, she already is. Just look at Skeeter!! (gales of laughter)

(The preceding was an actual court case heard in Houston, Texas, during March 1995. Bold print indicates what came out in the trial; plain print indicates the kinds of comments that might be made by others in generational poverty.)

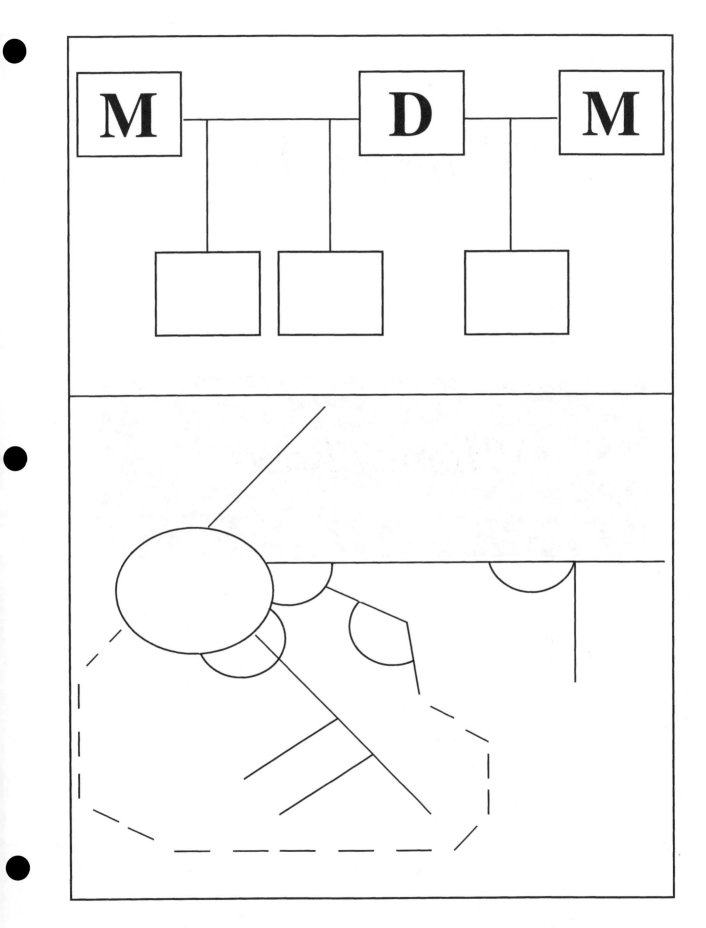

aha! Process, Inc. • (800) 424-9484

MODULE FIVE

HIDDEN RULES

COULD YOU SURVIVE IN POVERTY?

Put a check by each item you know how to do.

_____ 1.   I know which churches and sections of town have the best rummage sales.

_____ 2.   I know which rummage sales have "bag sales" and when.

_____ 3.   I know which grocery stores' garbage bins can be accessed for thrown-away food.

_____ 4.   I know how to get someone out of jail.

_____ 5.   I know how to physically fight and defend myself physically.

_____ 6.   I know how to get a gun, even if I have a police record.

_____ 7.   I know how to keep my clothes from being stolen at the Laundromat.

_____ 8.   I know what problems to look for in a used car.

_____ 9.   I know how to live without a checking account.

_____ 10.   I know how to live without electricity and a phone.

_____ 11.   I know how to use a knife as scissors.

_____ 12.   I can entertain a group of friends with my personality and my stories.

_____ 13.   I know what to do when I don't have money to pay the bills.

_____ 14.   I know how to move in half a day.

_____ 15.   I know how to get and use food stamps or an electronic card for benefits.

_____ 16.   I know where the free medical clinics are.

_____ 17.   I am very good at trading and bartering.

_____ 18.   I can get by without a car.

aha! Process, Inc. • (800) 424-9484

COULD YOU SURVIVE IN MIDDLE CLASS?

Put a check by each item you know how to do.

_____1.　I know how to get my children into Little League, piano lessons, soccer, etc.

_____2.　I know how to properly set a table.

_____3.　I know which stores are most likely to carry the clothing brands my family wears.

_____4.　My children know the best name brands in clothing.

_____5.　I know how to order in a nice restaurant.

_____6.　I know how to use a credit card, checking account, and savings account – and I understand an annuity. I understand term life insurance, disability insurance, and 20/80 medical insurance policy, as well as house insurance, flood insurance, and replacement insurance.

_____7.　I talk to my children about going to college.

_____8.　I know how to get one of the best interest rates on my new-car loan.

_____9.　I understand the difference among the principal, interest, and escrow statements on my house payment.

_____10.　I know how to help my children with their homework and do not hesitate to call the school if I need additional information.

_____11.　I know how to decorate the house for the different holidays.

_____12.　I know how to get a library card.

_____13.　I know how to use the different tools in the garage.

_____14.　I repair items in my house almost immediately when they break – or know a repair service and call it.

COULD YOU SURVIVE IN WEALTH?

Put a check by each item you know how to do.

_____1.   I can read a menu in French, English, and another language.

_____2.   I have several favorite restaurants in different countries of the world.

_____3.   During the holidays, I know how to hire a decorator to identify the appropriate themes and items with which to decorate the house.

_____4.   I know who my preferred financial advisor, legal service, designer, domestic-employment service, and hairdresser are.

_____5.   I have at least two residences that are staffed and maintained.

_____6.   I know how to ensure confidentiality and loyalty from my domestic staff.

_____7.   I have at least two or three "screens" that keep people whom I do not wish to see away from me.

_____8.   I fly in my own plane, the company plane, or the Concorde.

_____9.   I know how to enroll my children in the preferred private schools.

_____10.   I know how to host the parties that "key" people attend.

_____11.   I am on the boards of at least two charities.

_____12.   I know the hidden rules of the Junior League.

_____13.   I support or buy the work of a particular artist.

_____14.   I know how to read a corporate financial statement and analyze my own financial statements.

41

Hidden Rules

GENERATIONAL POVERTY	MIDDLE CLASS	WEALTH
◆ The driving forces for decision making are survival, relationships and entertainment.	◆ The driving forces for decision making are work and achievement.	◆ The driving forces for decision making are social, financial and political connections.
◆ People are possessions. It is worse to steal someone's girlfriend than a thing. A relationship is valued over achievement. That is why you must defend your child no matter what he or she has done. Too much education is feared because the individual might leave.	◆ Things are possessions. If material security is threatened, often the relationship is broken.	◆ Legacies, one-of-a-kind objects, and pedigrees are possessions.
◆ The "world" is defined in local terms.	◆ The "world" is defined in national terms. The national news is watched; travel tends to be in the nation.	◆ The "world" is defined in international terms.
◆ Physical fighting is how conflict is resolved. If you only know casual register, you do not have the words to negotiate a resolution. Respect is accorded to those who can physically defend themselves.	◆ Fighting is done verbally. Physical fighting is viewed with distaste.	◆ Fighting is done through social inclusion/exclusion and through lawyers.
◆ Food is valued for its quantity.	◆ Food is valued for its quality.	◆ Food is valued for its presentation.

Other Rules

◆ You laugh when you are disciplined; it is a way to save face. Your mother is the most important person in your life. Many times, the mother is the keeper of the soul. An insult against your mother is unforgivable.

◆ The noise level is higher, non-verbal information is more important than the verbal, emotions are openly displayed, and the value of your personality to the group is your ability to entertain.

◆ Destiny and fate govern. The notion of having choices is foreign. Discipline is about penance and forgiveness, not change.

◆ Tools are often not available. Therefore, the concept of repair and fixing may not be present.

◆ Formal register is always used in an interview and is often an expected part of social interaction.

◆ Work is a daily part of life.

◆ Discipline is about changing behavior. To stay in middle class, one must be self-governing and self-supporting.

◆ A reprimand is taken seriously (at least the pretense is there), without smiling and with some deference to authority.

◆ Choice is a key concept in the lifestyle. The future is very important. Formal education is seen as crucial for future success.

◆ The artistic and aesthetic are key to the lifestyle and include clothing, art, interior design, seasonal decorating, food, music, social activities, etc.

◆ For reasons of security and safety, virtually all contacts are dependent upon introductions (connections).

◆ Education is for the purpose of social, financial and political connections, as well as to enhance the artistic and aesthetic.

* One of the key differences between the well-to-do and the wealthy is that the wealthy almost always are patrons to the arts and often have an individual artist(s) to whom they are patrons as well.

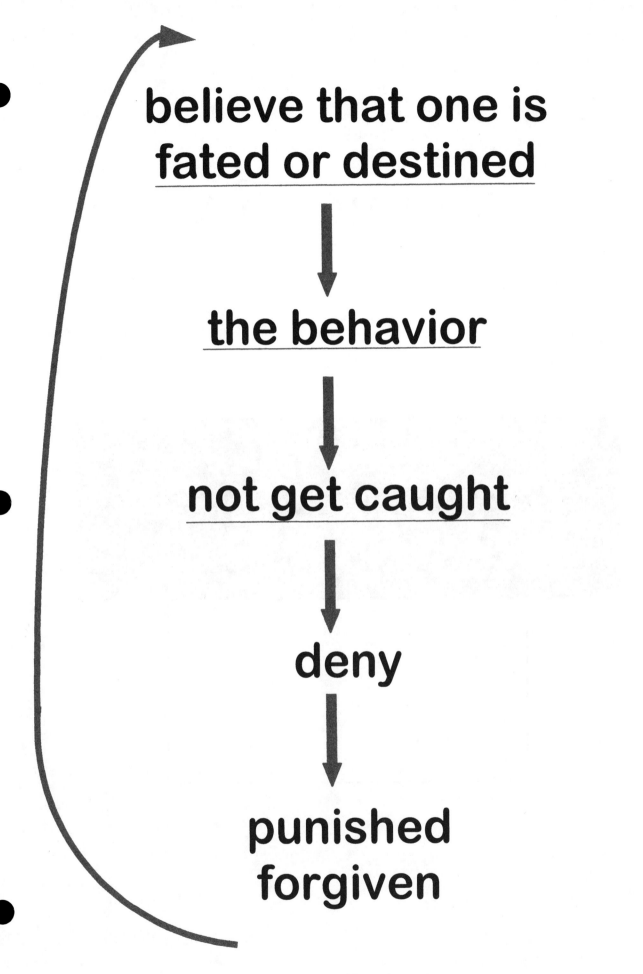

believe that one is
fated or destined

↓

the behavior

↓

not get caught

↓

deny

↓

punished
forgiven

43

MODULE SIX

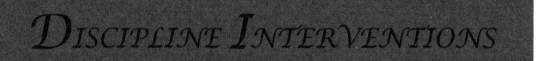

DISCIPLINE INTERVENTIONS

VOICES

CHILD

~ Quit picking on me.
~ You don't love me.
~ You want me to leave.
~ Nobody likes (loves) me.
~ I hate you.
~ You're ugly.
~ You make me sick.
~ It's your fault.
~ Don't blame me.
~ She, he, ... did it.
~ You make me mad.
~ You made me do it.

ADULT

~ In what ways could this be resolved?
~ What factors will be used to determine the effectiveness, quality of ....?
~ I would like to recommend ....
~ What are choices in this situation?
~ I am comfortable (uncomfortable) with ....
~ Options that could be considered, are ....
~ For me to be comfortable, I need the following things to occur ....
~ These are the consequences of that choice/action ....
~ We agree to disagree.

PARENT

~ You (shouldn't) should do that.
~ It's wrong (right) to do ....
~ That's stupid, immature, out of line, ridiculous.
~ Life's not fair. Get busy.
~ You are good, bad, worthless, beautiful (any judgmental, evaluative comment).
~ You do as I say.
~ If you weren't so ...., this wouldn't happen to you.
~ Why can't you be like ....?

aha! Process, Inc. • (800) 424-9484

Part three

Working With Students From Poverty: Discipline

By Ruby Payne, Ph.D.
Director of Professional Development, Goose Creek CISD

In poverty, discipline is often about penance and forgiveness. Because love is unconditional and because the time frame is the present, the notion that discipline should be instructive and change behavior is not a part of the culture in generational poverty. In matriarchal, generational poverty, the mother is the most powerful position and is in some ways "keeper of the soul." So she dispenses the judgments, determines the amount and price of penance, and gives forgiveness. When forgiveness is granted, behaviors and activities return to the way they were before the incident.

It is important to note that the approach is to teach a separate set of behaviors. Many of the behaviors students bring to school help them survive outside of school. Students learn and use many different rules depending on the Nintendo game they are playing. Likewise, they need to learn to use different rules to be successful in the setting they are in. If poor students do not know how to fight physically,

they are going to be in danger on the streets. But if that is their only method for resolving a problem, then they cannot be successful in school.

The culture of poverty does not provide for success in the middle class, because the middle class to a large extent requires the self-governance of behavior. To be successful in work and in school requires the self-governance of behavior. What then do schools need to do to teach appropriate behavior?

Structure and Choice

The two anchors of any effective discipline program that moves students to self-governance are structure and choice. The program must clearly outline the expected behaviors and the consequences of not choosing those

behaviors. The program must also emphasize that the individual always has choice—to follow or not to follow the expected behaviors. With each choice then comes consequence—either desirable or not desirable. Many discipline workshops use this approach and are available to schools.

When the focus is, "I'll tell you what to do and when," the student can never move from dependence to independence. He or she is always at the level of dependence.

Behavior Analysis

Mentally or in writing, teachers or administrators must first examine the behavior analysis:

1. Decide what behaviors the child needs to have to be successful.
2. Does the child have the

resources to develop those behaviors?

3. Will it help to contact a parent? Are resources available through them? What resources are available through the school district?

4. How will behaviors be taught?

5. What are other choices the child could make?

6. What will help the child repeat the successful behavior?

When these questions are completed, they provide answers to the strategies that will most help the student. The chart on the next page indicates possible explanations of behaviors and possible interventions.

Participation of the Student

While the teacher or administrator is analyzing, the

The culture of poverty does not provide for success in the middle class, because the middle class to a large extent requires the self-governance of behavior.

Behavior Related to Poverty	Intervention
Laughs when disciplined. A way to save face in matriarchal poverty.	*Understand the reason for the behavior. Tell the student three or four other behaviors that would be more appropriate.*
Argues loudly with the teacher. Poverty is participatory, and the culture has a distrust of authority. Sees the system as inherently dishonest and unfair.	*Don't argue with the student. Have them complete the four questions on page 4. Model respect for students.*
Angry response. Anger is based on fear. The question is what the fear is—loss of face?	*Respond in the adult voice. When the student cools down, discuss other responses that could be used.*
Inappropriate or vulgar comments. They rely on casual register, may not know formal register.	*Make students generate or teach students other phrases that could be used to say the same thing.*
Physically fights. Necessary to survive in poverty. Only knows the language of survival. Does not have language or belief system to use conflict resolution. Sees himself as less than a man if does not fight.	*Stress that fighting is unacceptable in school. Examine other options the student could live with at school. One option is not to settle the business at school.*
Hands always on someone else. Poverty has a heavy reliance on nonverbal data and touch.	*Allow them to draw or doodle. Have them hold their hands behind their backs when in line or standing. Give them as much to do with their hands as is possible in a constructive way.*
Cannot follow directions. Little procedural memory used in poverty. Sequence not used or valued.	*Write steps on the board. Have them write at the top of the paper the steps needed to finish the task. Have them practice procedural self-talk.*
Extremely disorganized. Lack of planning, scheduling or prioritizing skills. Not taught in poverty. Also, probably does not have a place to put things at home so they can be found.	*Teach a simple color-coded method of organization in the classroom. Use the five-finger method for memory at the end of the day. Make students give a plan for their own organization.*
Only completed part of a task. No procedural self-talk. Does not "see" the whole task.	*Write on the board all the parts of the task. Make students check off each part when finished.*
Disrespectful to teacher. Has lack of respect for authority and the system. May not know any adults worthy of respect.	*Tell students that approach is not a choice. Identify for students the correct voice tone and word choice that is acceptable. Make them practice.*
Harms other students, verbally or physically. This may be a way of life. Probably a way to buy space or distance. May have become a habitual response. Poverty tends to address issues in the negative.	*Tell the students that approach is not a choice. Have the students generate other options. Give students alternative verbal phrases.*
Cheats or steals. Indicative of weak support system, weak role models/emotional resources. May indicate extreme financial need. May indicate no instruction/ guidance during formative years.	*Use metaphor story to find the reason or need the cheating and stealing met. Address the reason or need. Stress that the behavior is illegal and not a choice at school.*
Constantly talks. Poverty is very participatory.	*Make students write all questions and responses on a note card two days a week. Tell students they get five comments a day. Build participatory activities into the lesson.*

student must analyze as well. To help students do so, give them this four-part questionnaire. This has been used with students as young as second semester, first grade. Students have the most difficulty with question number three. Basically, they see no other choices available than the one they have made.

In going over the sheet with the student, it is important to discuss other choices that could have been made. Students often do not have access to another way to deal with the situation. For example, if I slam my finger in the car door, I can cry, cuss, hit the car, be silent, kick the tire, laugh, stoically open the car door, groan, etc.

Name:
1. What did you do?
2. Why did you do that?
3. List four other things you could have done.
4. What will you do next time?

The Language of Negotiation

One of the bigger issues with students from poverty is that many of them are their own parents. They parent themselves and others—often younger siblings. In many instances, they are the parent to the adult in the household.

Inside everyone's head are internal voices that guide the individual. These three voices are referred to as the child voice, the adult voice and the parent voice. It has been my observation that individuals who have become their own parent quite young do not have an internal adult voice. They have a child voice and a parent voice, but not an adult voice.

What an internal adult voice does is allow for negotiation. This voice provides the language of negotiation and allows the issues to be

---

> **Educators tend to speak to students in a parent voice, particularly in discipline situations. To the student who is already functioning as a parent, this is unbearable, and almost immediately, the incident is exacerbated beyond the original happening.**

---

examined in a non-threatening way.

Educators tend to speak to students in a parent voice, particularly in discipline situations. To the student who is already functioning as a parent, this is unbearable, and almost immediately, the incident is exacerbated beyond the original happening. The tendency is for educators to also use the parent voice with poor parents because the assumption is that a lack of resources must indicate a lack of intelligence. Poor parents are extremely offended by this as well.

When the parent voice is used with a student who is already a parent in many ways, the outcome is anger. The student is angry because anger is based on fear. What the parent voice forces the student to do is either use the child voice or use the parent voice. If the student uses the parent voice, the student will get in trouble. If the student uses the child voice, he or she will feel helpless and therefore at the mercy of the adult. Many students choose to use the parent voice in return because it is less frightening than the memories connected with being helpless.

Part of the reality of poverty is the language of sur-

vival. There are simply not enough resources to engage in a discussion of them. For example, if there are five hot dogs and five people, the distribution of the food is fairly clear. The condiments for the hot dogs are going to be limited so the discussion will be fairly limited as well. So the ability to see options and to negotiate among those options is not well developed. Contrast that, for example, with a middle-class household where the discussion will be about how many hot dogs, what should go on the hot dog, etc.

To teach students to use the "language of negotiation," one must first teach them the phrases they can use. Especially, beginning in grade four, have them use the "adult" voice in discussions. Direct teach the notion of an adult voice and give them phrases to use. Make them tally each time they use a phrase from the "adult" voice. There will be laughter. However, over time, if teachers also model that voice in their interactions with students, they will hear more of those kinds of questions and statements.

In addition to this form, several staff development programs are available to

teach peer negotiation as well. It is important that as a part of the negotiation, the culture of origin is not denigrated, but rather the ability to negotiate is seen as a survival skill for the work and school setting.

CHILD
Defensive, victimized, emotional, whining, lose mentality, strong negative non-verbal.

Quit picking on me. You don't love me. You want me to leave. Nobody likes (loves) me. I hate you. You are ugly. You make me sick. It's your fault. Don't blame me. She (he) did it. You make me mad. You make me do it.

The child voice is also playful, spontaneous, curious, etc. These phrases listed occur in conflict or manipulative situations and impede resolution.

ADULT
Non-judgmental, free of negative nonverbal, factual, often in question format, attitude of win-win.

In what ways could this be resolved? What criteria will be used to determine the effectiveness and quality of.... I would like to recommend.... What are the choices in this situation? I am comfortable (uncomfortable) with.... Options that could be considered are.... For me to be comfortable, I need the following things to occur.... These are the consequences of that choice or action.... We agree to disagree.

PARENT

Authoritative, directive, judgmental, evaluative, win-lose mentality, advising, (sometimes threatening, demanding, punitive).

You should not (should) do that. It is wrong (right) to do that. I would advise you to.... That's stupid, immature, out of line, ridiculous. Life's not fair. Get busy. You are good, bad, worthless, beautiful (any judgmental, evaluative comment). You do as I say. If you weren't so..., this wouldn't happen to you.

The parent voice can also be very loving and supportive. These phrases listed occur during conflict and impede resolution. The internal parent voice can create shame and guilt.

Using Metaphor Stories

Another technique for working with students and adults is to use a metaphor story. A metaphor story will help an individual voice issues that affects their actions.

A metaphor story does not have any proper names in it. For example, a student keeps going to the nurse's office two or three times a week. There is nothing wrong with her, yet she keeps going.

Adult to Jennifer, the girl:

"Jennifer, I am going to tell a story and I need you to help me. It is about a fourth-grade girl much like yourself. I need you to help me tell the story because I am not in the fourth grade. Once upon a time, there was a girl who went to the nurse's office. Why did the girl go to the nurse's office? (Because she thought there was something wrong with her.) So the girl went to the nurse's office because she thought there was something wrong with her. Did the nurse find anything wrong with her. (No, the nurse did not.) So the nurse did not find anything wrong with her, yet the girl kept going to the nurse. Why did the girl keep going to the nurse? (Because she thought there was something wrong with her.) So the girl thought something was wrong with her. Why did the girl think there was something wrong with her? (She saw a TV show....)"

The story continues until the reason for the behavior is found and then the story needs to end on a positive note. "So, she went to the doctor, and he gave her tests and found that she was OK."

This is an actual case. What came out in the story was that Jennifer had seen a TV show in which a girl her age had died suddenly and had never known she was ill. Jennifer's parents took her to the doctor. He ran tests and told her she was fine. She did not go to the nurse's office

anymore.

A metaphor story is to be used one-on-one when there is a need to understand the behavior and what is needed is to move the student to the appropriate behavior.

Teaching Hidden Rules

For example, if a student from poverty laughs when he is disciplined, the teacher needs to say, "Do you use the same rules to play all Nintendo games? No, you don't because you would lose. The same is true at school. There are street rules and there are school rules. Each set of rules helps you be successful where you are. So, at school, laughing when disciplined is not a choice. It does not help you to be successful. It only buys you more trouble. Keep a straight face and look contrite, even if you aren't."

That is an example of teaching a hidden rule. It can even be more straightforward with older students. "Look, there are hidden rules on the street and hidden rules at school. What are they?" And then after the discussion, detail the rules that make the student successful where they are.

What Does This Information Mean in the School or Work Setting?

• Students from poverty need to have at least two sets of behaviors from which to

choose—one set for the streets, and one set for school and work.

• The purpose of discipline should be to promote successful behaviors at school.

• Teaching students to use the adult voice, i.e. the language of negotiation, is important for their success in and out of school and can become an alternative to physical aggression.

• Structure and choice need to be a part of the discipline approach.

• Discipline should be a form of instruction.

AUTHOR NOTE:
Ruby K. Payne, Ph.D., is the director of professional development at Goose Creek CISD in Baytown, Texas. She is also the author of *Poverty: A Framework for Understanding and Working With Students and Adults from Poverty.* Contact her by phone at 713-424-9151 and by fax at 713-424-2297.

Students from poverty need to have at least two sets of behaviors from which to choose—one set for the streets, and one set for school and work.

MODULE SEVEN

BUILDING RELATIONSHIPS

creating relationships

DEPOSITS	WITHDRAWALS
Seek first to understand	Seek first to be understood
Keeping promises	Breaking promises
Kindnesses, courtesies	Unkindnesses, discourtesies
Clarifying expectations	Violating expectations
Loyalty to the absent	Disloyalty, duplicity
Apologies	Pride, conceit, arrogance
Open to feedback	Rejecting feedback
Chart taken from Stephen Covey's book ...	*The Seven Habits of Highly Effective People*

DEPOSITS MADE TO INDIVIDUAL IN POVERTY	WITHDRAWALS MADE FROM INDIVIDUAL IN POVERTY
Appreciation for humor and entertainment provided by the individual	Put-downs or sarcasm about the humor or the individual
Acceptance of what the individual cannot say about a person or situation	Insistence and demands for full explanation about a person or situation
Respect for the demands and priorities of relationships	Insistence on the middle-class view of relationships
Using the adult voice	Using the parent voice
Assisting with goal-setting	Telling the individual his/her goals
Identifying options related to available resources	Making judgments on the value and availability of resources
Understanding the importance of personal freedom, speech, and individual personality	Assigning pejorative character traits to the individual

51

aha! Process, Inc. • (800) 424-9484

What are things a teacher can do to build relationships?

TESA (Teacher Expectations and Student Achievement) identified 15 behaviors that teachers use with good students. The research study found that when teachers used these interactions with low-achieving students, their achievement made significant gains.

The teacher ...

1. calls on everyone in the room equitably.
2. provides individual help.
3. gives "wait" time (allows student enough time to answer).
4. asks questions to give the student clues about the answer.
5. asks questions that require more thought.
6. tells students whether their answers are right or wrong.
7. gives specific praise.
8. gives reasons for praise.
9. listens.
10. accepts feelings of the student.
11. gets within an arm's reach of each student each day.
12. is courteous to students.
13. shows personal interest and gives compliments.
14. touches students (appropriately).
15. desists (he/she does not call attention to every negative behavior).

MODULE EIGHT

DEVELOPING EMOTIONAL RESOURCES

BUILDING EMOTIONAL RESOURCES

To build emotional resources, structure, choice and adult voice must be used. Furthermore, the student must have a relationship, or mutual respect, with the adult. To be able to build emotional resources in students, an understanding of these topics is helpful:

1) emotional intelligence (EQ)
2) emotional blackmail
3) resiliency
4) emotional coaching
5) coping strategies
6) use of stories

Emotional intelligence is the ability to respond emotionally to a situation from choice without doing harm to yourself or others. A short quiz is included to assess your emotional intelligence (page 61-63). Emotional blackmail is when fear, guilt or obligation is used to manipulate you into a behavior(s). Resiliency is the research that examines the seven personal characteristics that individuals develop that allows them to move out of dysfunctional and damaging situations. Emotional coaching is the approach that helps develop emotional intelligence. Coping strategies are specific things a person can say or do with students to help them develop resilient characteristics and deal with a given situation. Stories can be used to teach concepts and behaviors.

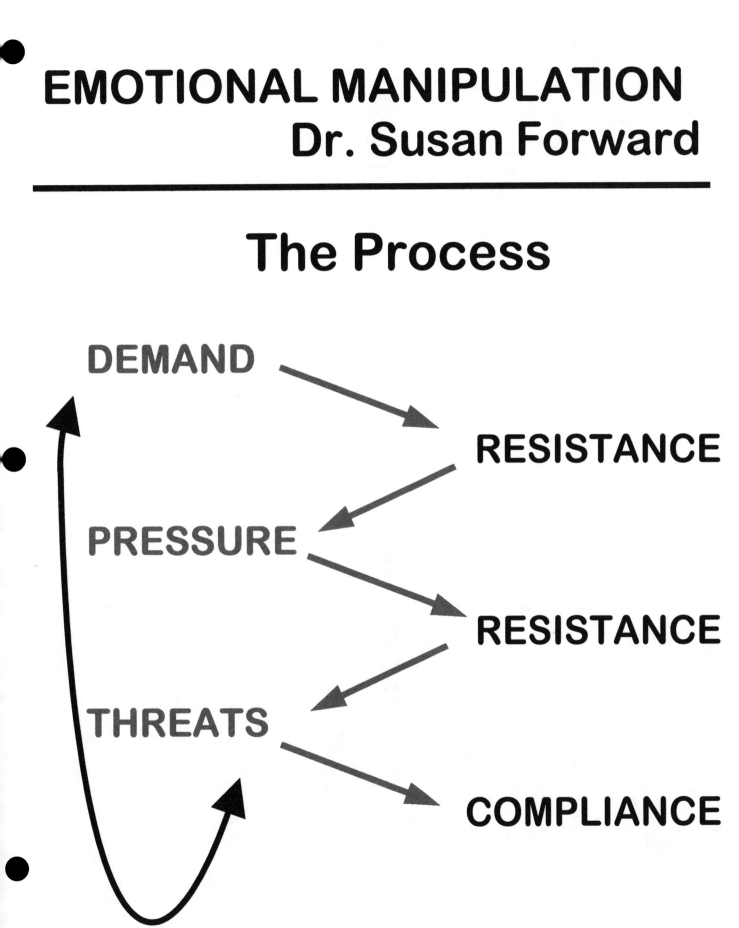

EMOTIONAL MANIPULATION
Dr. Susan Forward

The Process

DEMAND

RESISTANCE

PRESSURE

RESISTANCE

THREATS

COMPLIANCE

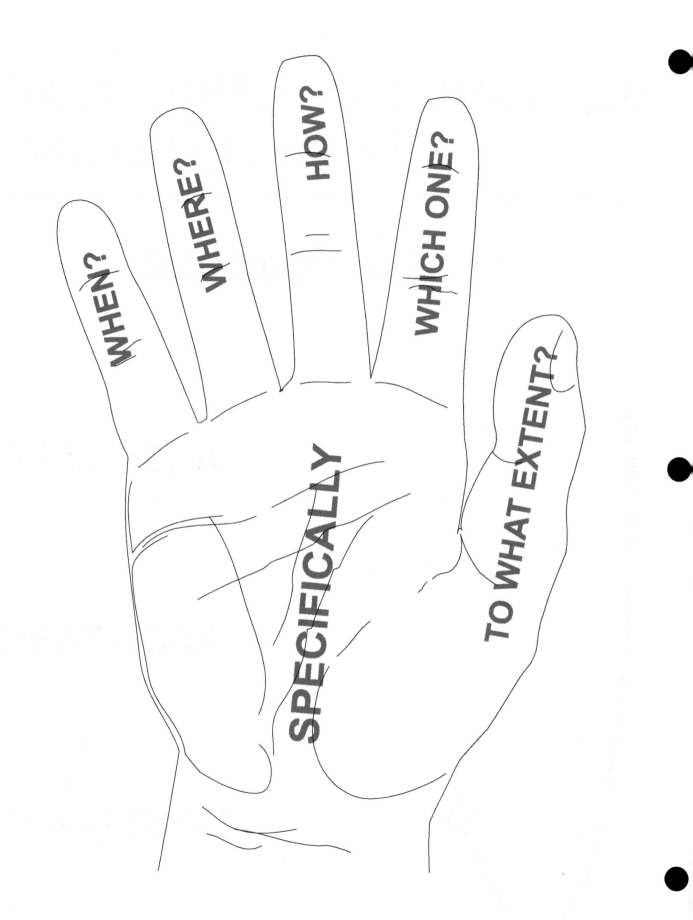

STOPPING EMOTIONAL MANIPULATION

Stop:

> DO NOTHING.
> BUY TIME.
> ACCEPT DISCOMFORT.
> GET EMOTIONAL DISTANCE AND SPACE.

Observe:

> STEP BACK.
> 1. WHAT HAPPENED?
> 2. WHAT WAS MY SELF-TALK?
> 3. HOW DID I FEEL?
> 4. WHAT ARE MY "FLASHPOINTS" OR "TRIGGERS"?

Strategize:

> IDENTIFY THE DEMAND
> 1. NO BIG DEAL
> 2. IMPORTANT ISSUE INVOLVING INTEGRITY
> 3. MASTER LIFE ISSUE
>
> FOUR STRATEGIES
> 1. USE ADULT VOICE (BE NON-DEFENSIVE)
> 2. SEEK TO UNDERSTAND / "I WONDER"
> 3. BARTERING (COMPROMISE)
> 4. HUMOR

aha! Process, Inc. • (800) 424-9484

HOW TO HANDLE EMOTIONAL MANIPULATION

What is emotional manipulation?

It is simply when an individual tries to force a certain behavior in another by manipulating feelings, primarily through the parent voice or child voice.

Often in poverty, the attack is personal. In affluence, the attack is on the issue, professional approaches, and responsibility. The book *Emotional Blackmail*, by Susan Forward, identifies these types of "blackmailers." Responses to blackmail include: anger, attempt to fix the problem, acquiescence, blaming, war, and avoidance.

What techniques are used?

Criticism, flattery, "help me," withdrawal of love or support, anger, absence, silence, accusation.

How do you respond to emotional manipulation?

Here are some basic rules of thumb.

1. Stay in the adult voice.

2. It is their perception and approach, not yours.

3. You choose your reaction. If you respond in kind, you have let them make your choice.

4. Use such phrases as the following from the ensuing examples.

    Example:

    A parent says to you, "You don't like my child. You're prejudiced."

    You say, "What happened, specifically, to make you believe that?"

    Parent says, "My son told me. I believe him."

    You say, "I need to know what happened, specifically, that makes him think that."

    Parent says, "He don't have to give you no specifics."

    You say, "How can I help solve the problem without knowing, specifically, what happened?"

    (Giving the parent a way out of the corner. The parent realizes at this point that he or she is trapped.)

    You say, "What do you think would help to solve the problem? And you can be specific?"

    Parent says, "Nothing. You're no good."

You say,   "I know you love and care about your child very much, or you wouldn't be here. If you can provide me with specific ways to help, I would like to hear them." If the parent persists, say, "I'm sorry but this conversation is not helping your child."

HOW NOT TO HANDLE IT.

Example:

Parent says,   "You don't like my child. You're prejudiced."

You say,   "That is just his opinion. Do you believe everything he tells you? One thing I learned from my children is that ... "

Parent says,   "My son told me. I believe him."

You say,   "You might want to check your sources. He lies, you know. What did he say specifically?"

Parent says,   "I don't have to give you no specifics."

You say,   "Yes, you do. Otherwise you can leave. I don't have to listen to your insults."

HOW TO HANDLE IT (when a parent wants a grade changed, etc.)

Example:

Parent says,   "I really question the way you arrived at your grades. My sister is a teacher and I asked her, and she says no respectable professional figures grades this way."

You say,   "Let me show you the method I use. I have color-coded my gradebook. These are the percentages I give; these were the assignments that were given."

Parent says,   "Well, I don't agree with that method. Why did you decide that 25% of the final grade goes to the six-weeks exam?"

You say,   "That is board policy."

Parent says,   "I want to see that test." (You provide test. Parent criticizes test. Then parent asks about assignments, criticizes these.)

You say,   "It seems the real issue is his grade. What grade did you want him to receive?"

59   aha! Process, Inc. • (800) 424-9484

Parent says,   "He should have had an A. He's the brightest one in his class."

You say nothing, just wait quietly.

Parent says,   "If you asked for the level of work in keeping with his ability, then you would see the difference. This work is Mickey Mouse stuff. He doesn't do it because he's bored."

You say nothing, just wait quietly.

Parent says,   "Well, aren't you going to say anything? Lost your ability to speak?"

You say,   "I know you love and care about your son very much or you wouldn't be here. Changing his grade will not help him be more successful. We could use this situation as a way to give him coping strategies that will increase his success. I would like for us to work together and monitor his success for the coming six weeks in this way ... "

Parent says,   "OK."

PHRASES

Student says,   "You can't make me do that."

Response,   "You're right. I can't. You can choose to do the assignment, or you can choose to go to the office, detention, etc."

Student says,   "I'm going to tell my mama."

Response,   "Good. I will talk to her also."

Student says,   "You're a bitch."

Response,   "I'm sorry you feel that way."

Student says,   "You don't like me."

Response,   "I don't always like what you do. But I care about you very much."

What's Your Emotional Intelligence Quotient?
You'll Soon Find Out ...
Source: The Internet (http://www.utne.com/lens/bms/eq.html)

The following questions will give you a rough sense of what your EQ might be. Answer honestly, on the basis of what you really would be most likely to do. (Don't try to second-guess what seems right by using those old rules for psyching out multiple-choice tests that helped you through school!)

1. You're on an airplane that suddenly hits extremely bad turbulence and begins rocking from side to side. What do you do?
    A. Continue to read your book, magazine, or watch the movie, paying little attention to the turbulence.
    B. Become vigilant for an emergency, carefully monitoring the stewardesses and reading the emergency instructions card.
    C. A little of both A and B.
    D. Not sure – never noticed.

2. You've taken a group of 4-year-olds to the park, and one of them starts crying because the others won't play with her. What do you do?
    A. Stay out of it – let the kids deal with it on their own.
    B. Talk to her and help her figure out ways to get the other kids to play with her.
    C. Tell her in a kind voice not to cry.
    D. Try to distract the crying girl by showing her some other things she could play with.

3. Assume you're a college student who had hoped to get an A in a course, but you have just found out you got a C- on the midterm. What do you do?
    A. Sketch out a specific plan for ways to improve your grade and resolve to follow through on your plans.
    B. Resolve to do better in the future.
    C. Tell yourself it really doesn't matter much how you do in the course, concentrating instead on other classes where your grades are higher.
    D. Go to see the professor and try to talk her into giving you a better grade.

4. Imagine you're an insurance salesman calling prospective clients. Fifteen people in a row have hung up on you, and you're getting discouraged. What do you do?
    A. Call it a day and hope you have better luck tomorrow.
    B. Assess qualities in yourself that may be undermining your ability to make a sale.
    C. Try something new in the next call; keep plugging away.
    D. Consider another line of work.

5. You're a manager in an organization that is trying to encourage respect for racial and ethnic diversity. You overhear someone telling a racist joke. What do you do?
    A. Ignore it – it's only a joke.
    B. Call the person into your office for a reprimand.
    C. Speak up on the spot, saying that such jokes are inappropriate and will not be tolerated in your organization.
    D. Suggest to the person telling the joke that he go through a diversity training program.

61

6. You're trying to calm down a friend who has worked himself up into a fury at a driver in another car who has cut dangerously close in front of him. What do you do?
   A. Tell him to forget it – he's OK now and it's no big deal.
   B. Put on one of his favorite tapes and try to distract him.
   C. Join him putting down the other driver, as a show of rapport.
   D. Tell him about a time something like this happened to you and how you felt as mad as he does now, but then you saw that the other driver was on the way to a hospital emergency room.

7. You and your life partner have gotten into an argument that has escalated into a shouting match; you're both upset and, in the heat of anger, make personal attacks you don't really mean. What's the best thing to do?
   A. Take a 20-minute break, then continue the discussion.
   B. Just stop the argument – go silent, no matter what your partner says.
   C. Say you're sorry and ask your partner to apologize, too.
   D. Stop for a moment, collect your thoughts, and state your side of the case as precisely as you can.

8. You've been assigned to head a working team that is trying to come up with a creative solution to a nagging problem at work. What's the best thing to do?
   A. Draw up an agenda and allot time for discussion of each item so you make best use of your time together.
   B. Have people take the time to get to know each other better.
   C. Begin by asking each person for ideas about how to solve the problem, while the ideas are fresh.
   D. Start out with a brainstorming session, encouraging everyone to say whatever comes to mind, no matter how wild.

9. Your 3-year-old son is extremely timid and has been hypersensitive about – and a bit fearful of – new places and people virtually since he was born. What do you do?
   A. Accept that he has a shy temperament and think of ways to shelter him from situations that would upset him.
   B. Take him to a child psychiatrist for help.
   C. Purposely expose him to lots of new people and places so he can get over his fear.
   D. Engineer an ongoing series of challenging but manageable experiences that will teach him he can handle new people and places.

10. For years you've wanted to get back to learning to play a musical instrument that you tried in childhood, and now, just for fun, you've finally gotten around to starting. You want to make the most effective use of your time. What do you do?
    A. Hold yourself to a strict practice time each day.
    B. Choose pieces that stretch your abilities a bit.
    C. Practice only when you're really in the mood.
    D. Pick pieces that are far beyond your ability, but that you can master with diligent effort.

To Score Your Test ...

Assign the point value to your answer for each question. Add together all your points. The meaning of your score (hypothetically) is below.

1. A = 20; B = 20; C = 20; D = 0
   Anything but D—that answer reflects a lack of awareness of your habitual responses under stress.

2. A = 0; B = 20; C = 0; D = 0
   B.   Emotionally intelligent parents use their children's moments of upsets as opportunities to act as emotional coaches, helping their children understand what got them upset, what they are feeling, and alternatives the children can try.

3. A = 20; B = 0; C = 0; D = 0
   A.   One mark of self-motivation is being able to formulate a plan for overcoming obstacles and frustrations and following through on it.

4. A = 0; B = 20; C = 20; D = 0
   C.   Optimism, a mark of emotional intelligence, leads people to see setbacks as challenges they can learn from, and to persist, trying out new approaches rather than giving up, blaming themselves, or getting demoralized.

5. A = 0; B = 0; C = 20; D = 0
   C.   The most effective way to create an atmosphere that welcomes diversity is to make clear in public that the social norms of your organization do not tolerate such expressions. Instead of trying to change prejudices (a much harder task), keep people from acting on them.

6. A = 0; B = 5; C = 5; D = 20
   D.   Data on rage and how to calm it show the effectiveness of distracting the angry person from the focus of his rage, empathizing with his feelings and perspective, and suggesting a less anger-provoking way of seeing the situation.

7. A = 20; B = 0; C = 0; D = 0
   A.   Take a break of 20 minutes or more. It takes at least that long to clear the body of the physiological arousal of anger – which distorts your perception and makes you more likely to launch damaging personal attacks. After cooling down, you'll be more likely to have a fruitful discussion.

8. A = 0; B = 20; C = 0; D = 0
   B.   Creative groups work at their peak when rapport, harmony, and comfort levels are highest – then people are freer to make their best contribution.

9. A = 0; B = 5; C = 0; D = 20
   D.   Children born with a timid temperament can often become more outgoing if their parents arrange an ongoing series of manageable challenges to their shyness.

10. A = 0; B = 20; C = 0; D = 0
    B.   By giving yourself moderate challenges, you are most likely to get into the state of flow, which is both pleasurable and where people learn and perform at their best.

200 – Genius	125 – Freud	50 – Emotionally challenged
175 – Empathetic	100 – Average	25 – Neanderthal
150 – Gandhi	75 – Have you tried psychotherapy	

Little Eight John

A family who used to live next door to Ms. Emma had a whole brood of boys. They named the first boy John, after his father. Everybody called that child Junior. They named the second boy John, after his father, and everybody called that child Trey. They had five more boys, and they named them all John, after their father. Those boys had nicknames, too: Red and Bubba, Gordie and Slim, and one called Mohammed. I can't remember which was which. After their eighth boy, they quit. The last one they called Little Eight John. He was named after his brothers.

Most of those boys were good boys and didn't worry their mother. But Little Eight John was bad to the bone. If his mama told him to do one thing, he would do just the opposite and then think it was funny! If his mama told him not to step on the toads because it would bring bad luck to the family, he would race out the door and stomp those little toads flat, all the while laughing at his own mischief.

When the car wouldn't start, or the TV went out, the family blamed Little Eight John because of the toad squashing. He just laughed and laughed. His mama would say, "Little Eight John, don't sit backwards in your chair; it will bring troubles down on this household." Little Eight John would sit backwards in every chair in the house. In the afternoon, when the cornbread burned and the beans got scorched, everyone knew it was Eight John's fault. Little Eight John thought it was hysterical.

If you think Little Eight John was bad at home, you should have seen him at school. He ran in the halls, he talked without raising his hand, he sneaked food into class, and he never did his homework. He laughed at the teacher when she corrected him and told the principal the pops he gave didn't hurt a bit.

"You might as well give me two more," he said in the office. "It will save you the trouble the next time I come down."

He was so bad, they stuck him away in one of those special-behavior classes before he finished first grade. Even then, some days he got suspended and had to stay home and worry his mama.

"Don't count your teeth," his mother told Eight John, "or a sickness will come on your family." But Little Eight John went right ahead and counted his uppers and his lowers. He counted his teeth every day, once with his finger and once with his tongue. When his mama got migraine headaches and his brother Bubba got fever, Little Eight John got the giggles.

I mean to tell you, this boy was rotten. His mother would warn him, "Don't sleep with your head at the foot of the bed or you will bring the weary-money blues right into this house." So Little Eight John slept with his head at the foot of every bed in the house. Sure enough, late in the month someone robbed Little Eight John's mama, and she didn't have enough money to pay the water bill. Little Eight John thought it was funny when the water got cut off. He liked being dirty.

It got so bad that Little Eight John wouldn't even behave in church. On Sunday mornings he moaned and groaned about the length of the sermon and the choice of the songs. One Sunday he was caught stealing money from the offering plate. His mama pleaded with him to be good.

"If you don't mend your ways, the Devil himself is going to come after you."

Little Eight John didn't listen to one thing his mother said. One Sunday morning, after pretending to be deathly ill and unable to attend church, he was home alone playing, and the Devil did come after Little Eight John. He caught Little Eight John standing on the kitchen table and turned him into a grease spot right there next to the burn mark from the iron.

That was the end of Little Eight John, and that's what happens to children who don't mind what their mamas say. At least that's what Little Eight John's mama told his seven surviving brothers after prayer at Sunday dinner.

QUESTIONS FOR
STUDENT DISCUSSION
ON LITTLE EIGHT JOHN

1. Is it possible for someone to be born bad?

   Are you fated? In other words, can you do anything to change yourself, or are you destined to be the way you are?

   If you cannot make changes, then what is your life about?

   If you can make changes, why would you?

2. Do you believe that you can make choices then change?

3. Is it true that if you count your teeth, a sickness will come upon your family?

   What are superstitions? Do they come true?

   What superstitions have you heard in your neighborhood?

4. When a person makes choices and changes about who he or she is, does he or she lose friends?

5. Why is it hard to make changes in yourself? What are some things about yourself that you would like to change?

COPING STRATEGIES

Coping Strategies

1. Procedure

2. If ... Then

3. Bracketing

4. Metaphor Stories

5. Peer (Buddy)

6. Writing a Letter

7. Reframing

8. Self-Talk (I Do the Task for Me)

9. Goal-Setting

10. Helping Another Student

11. Homework Period

12. Replacement Behaviors

 aha! Process, Inc. • (800) 424-9484

RESILIENCY RESEARCH

Insight	*Tough Questions— Honest Answers: WHY?*
Independence	*Keeping Distance Emotionally and Physically*
Relationships	*Ties to People of Mutual Respect*
Initiative	*Taking Charge of Problems, Stretching Themselves*
Creativity	*Imposing Order, Beauty, Purpose*
Humor	*Finding the Comic in the Tragic*
Morality	*Staying Holy in an Unholy Place*

Adapted from *The Resilient Self: How Survivors of Troubled Families Rise Above Adversity,* by Wolins

Questions to Ask Students to Build Resiliency

Insight

Why?

Independence

How am I different?
How is this situation not about me?

Relationships

With whom do I have mutual respect?

Initiative

What can I do?
What parts can I address?

Creativity

What is my purpose?
What are the rules here?

Humor

What about this is funny?

Morality

What is the right thing to do?
What is humane, kind, compassionate?
What is the least destructive way to handle it?

aha! Process, Inc. • (800) 424-9484

A Legacy of Stability

Children raised by parents who are "emotion coaches" learn to trust their feelings, regulate their own emotions, and solve problems, says psychologist John Gottman. The emotion coach:

- **Is aware of and values his or her own emotions.**

- **Tolerates a sad, angry, or fearful child.**

- **Is sensitive to even subtle emotional states.**

- **Respects a child's emotions.**

- **Does not dictate how a child should feel.**

- **Does not need to fix a child's every problem.**

- **Uses emotional moments to achieve intimacy.**

John Gottman is the author of the book *The Heart of Parenting: Raising an Emotionally Intelligent Child.*

This was excerpted from an article in *USA Today.*

MODULE NINE

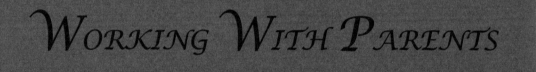

WORKING WITH PARENTS

WORKING WITH PARENTS FROM POVERTY

The first issue to address when working with parents from poverty is mutual respect. The second is the use of casual register. The third is the way discipline is used in the household. The fourth is the way time is viewed. And the fifth is the role of school and education in their lives.

First of all, for many parents in generational poverty, school is not given a high priority. It is often feared and resented. Their own personal experience may not have been positive and school is alternately viewed as a babysitter or a necessary evil (i.e., if I don't send my child, I will have to go to court). Second, when parents come in, because of their heavy reliance on win/lose approach to conflict, they may begin with an in-your-face approach. Remember, they are using this as a show of strength. Just stay in the adult voice. Use language that is clear and straightforward. If you use "educationese," they will think you are trying to cheat or trick them.

Use these kinds of phrases with parents: "Learning this will help your child win more often." … "The mind is a mental weapon that no one can take from you." … "Learning this information will keep your child from getting cheated or tricked." … "Learning this will help your child make more money." … "This information will help your child stay safer." Another thing to say to parents is: "I know you love and care about your child very much, or you wouldn't be here" (but don't say this if you don't mean it).

Discipline in generational poverty vacillates from being very permissive to very punitive. The emotional mood of the moment often determines what occurs. Also, in some cultures, the approach to boys is very different from the approach to girls. When the discipline is highly punitive, there is often a belief system that (a) the harsher the punishment, the greater the forgiveness, and (b) the harsher punishment will make the young person stronger and tougher. Consequently, the notion of a systematic approach to discipline often does not exist. There is rarely mediation about a behavior. Generally, it is a slap and a "Quit that." If guidance is being provided to the parent about behavior, use a WHAT, WHY, HOW approach with visuals. (See example, p. 74.)

GETTING PARENTS TO SCHOOL

One of the big difficulties for many schools is simply getting the parents into the school setting. Howard Johnson, a researcher at Southern Florida University, has done work with why urban parents come to school. The first reason they usually come is a crisis. What he has found is that rarely do they come to the school for reasons that school people think is important. So the first question that must be asked when trying to get parents to school is: "What's in it for the parents?"

A study done by the U.S. government in 1993 with Chapter I schools looked only at schools that were 75% low-income or more. Administrators of the study then identified students within those schools who achieved and students who did not. They developed a questionnaire looking at criteria in and out of school to understand the variables that made a difference in achievement.

Interestingly enough, whether parents actually went to school or attended meetings at school was not a significant factor. What made the biggest difference was whether or not parents provided three things for their children: support, insistence and expectations.

SOME SUGGESTIONS

1. Rather than use the meeting format, use the museum format. That way parents can come and go when it is convenient for their schedule. In other words, the school would be open from 6:00 to 9:00 p.m. Parents could come to this room to watch a video. The video would be repeated every half hour. Another room could have a formal meeting at a given time. Another room could have board games for the students. Another room could have food.

2. HAVE FOOD. Give gift certificates to grocery stores. These tend to be popular. Another favorite is clothes baskets that have soap, shampoo, perfumes, etc., because food stamps don't always allow those purchases.

3. Let the children come with the parents – for several reasons. First of all, there often is jealousy by the husband when his wife goes out alone. If the woman's children are with her, there is none. Second, school buildings often are big and confusing to parents. If the children go with them, the children help them find their way around. Third, a babysitter frequently is not available. And fourth, children are natural icebreakers. Parents tend to meet each other through their children.

4. Have classes that benefit parents. For example: how to speak and write English; how to fill out a job application; how to get a Social Security card; how to make money mowing yards, doing child care, baking and repairing small engines. Also, schools can make their computer labs available on Saturdays to teach things like CAD (computer-aided design) and word processing – simple introductory courses that last four or five Saturdays for a couple of hours.

ALTERNATIVE APPROACHES

1. Use video. Virtually every home in poverty has a TV and a VCR, even if it has very little else. Keep the videos under 15 minutes.

2. For all flyers home, use both visual and verbal information. (See example, p. 74.)

3. Provide simple, how-to activities that parents can do with children.

 aha! Process, Inc. • (800) 424-9484

TO DISCIPLINE YOUR CHILD/ STUDENT USE THESE STEPS.

1. **STOP** the behavior that is inappropriate.

2. Tell the child **WHAT** he/she did that was wrong.

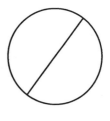

3. Tell the child **WHY** the behavior was wrong
   And its consequences.

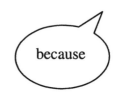

4. Tell the child **HOW** to behave the next time.

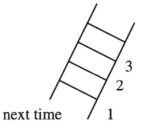

This is a note Ruby Payne received from an assistant principal:

I attended the Train the Trainers session in Houston in July. It was great. At the time, I had no idea how useful it was going to be when I was placed as assistant principal for the first time.

I am having a hard time in this school because there is a problem I've never had to deal with. It sounds like something Ruby might be able to shed some light on, but I don't remember her covering it at the session. A large number of parents in this school beat their children when I send a note or call home about the students' behaviors. I have had to call DHR many days after punishing a child. The staff is as overwhelmed as I am. They say this has not been a large problem until just recently. Many are holding back on sending them to the office because of fear of how the parents will handle the child afterward. All of us are anxious for some guidance. Can you give us some information or recommend some sources where we can do some reading? We pray for both Ruby and divine guidance. You can e-mail me here at school or at home.

Ruby's response:

It was great to hear from you and learn that the training was helpful.

Yes, about beating children. That is a very common response in generational poverty, particularly in Caucasian and African American settings. It is not as much of a pattern in Hispanic generational poverty, unless there are multiple relationships.

There are several reasons why parents beat their children. First, many times the parents only have two choices as well – a parent and a child voice. To move a child to self-governance, a person needs to have an adult voice so that the child can examine choices. Many parents cannot do this because they don't have an adult voice. So they use the parent voice. And in conflict, the parent voice tends to be a very harsh, punitive voice.

The second reason they beat their children is that typically they don't know any other approach. Usually raised themselves under punitive parenting, they believe the maxim that to spare the rod is to spoil the child.

The third reason is that it is part of the penance-forgiveness ritual. If you believe you are fated, then you really cannot change your behavior. So the greater the penance, the greater the forgiveness. You will often find that after parents beat their children (penance) they engage in a ritual of forgiveness. Forgiveness can include any or all of the following: cooking them their favorite meal; permissiveness; and giving them alcohol, cigarettes, part of the drug stash, and money. Or they might even come to school and chew someone out just to show their child that he or she is forgiven. The thinking is the following:

I do the behavior because I am fated; I cannot change who I am.
If I'm fated, then I can't really change what I do.
If I can't change what I do, then the real crime is in getting caught.

aha! Process, Inc. • (800) 424-9484

But if I get caught, then I'm going to deny it.
Because if I deny it, I might not get punished.
However, if I do get punished, then I also have gotten forgiven.
And I'm free to do the behavior again.

I have some suggestions for you.

First of all, I would approach the situation differently. When an incident occurs, I would call the parent and say, "I need your help. We are asking that you use a WHAT, WHY, HOW approach to discipline, which will help us here at school. That is what <u>we</u> are doing. When your child does something you don't like, please tell him WHAT he did, WHY it was not OK, and HOW to do it right. <u>We want him to win every time and be smarter at school</u>. So to help us, please use the WHAT, WHY, HOW approach. (As a reference point for yourself and parents, make a little brochure or paper with this approach clearly shown.) Then say, "Please do not hit him. When you hit him, we are required by law to call DHR. We don't want to have to do that. So please help us."

Parents are doing what they believe to be the right thing. Some will say to you, "Honey, you do what you have to at school, and we'll do what we have to at home."

Then you say, "I know you love and care about your child very much or you wouldn't be taking the time to talk to me. But I need your help, and I know you don't want me to call DHR. So, for anything having to do with school, please use the WHAT, WHY, HOW approach. It's a simple 1-2-3 deal. It's not easy being a parent, and we want you to be able to <u>win</u> as a parent. So please help us."

For the parents for whom this doesn't work, I would not call home anymore. I would look more for positive reinforcements than negative reinforcements. There is nothing we can do at school that is as negative as some of the stuff that happens outside of school.

Please stay in touch, and let me know how things are going.

BIBLIOGRAPHY

Berliner, D.C. (1988). *Implications of Studies of Expertise in Pedagogy for Teacher Education and Evaluation*. Paper presented at 1988 Educational Testing Service Invitational Conference on New Directions for Teacher Assessment. New York, NY.

Bloom, Benjamin. (1976). *Human Characteristics and School Learning*. New York, NY: McGraw-Hill Book Company.

Caine, Renate Nummela, & Caine, Geoffrey. (1991). *Making Connections: Teaching and the Human Brain*. Alexandria, VA: Association of Supervision and Curriculum Development.

Collins, Bryn C. (1997). *Emotional Unavailability: Recognizing It, Understanding It, and Avoiding Its Trap*. Lincolnwood, IL: NTC/Contemporary Publishing Company.

Covey, Stephen R. (1989). *The Seven Habits of Highly Effective People: Powerful Lessons in Personal Change*. New York, NY: Simon & Schuster.

Feuerstein, Reuven, et al. (1980). *Instrumental Enrichment: An Intervention Program for Cognitive Modifiability*. Glenview, IL: Scott, Foresman & Co.

Forward, Susan, with Frazier, Donna. (n.d.). *Emotional Blackmail*. New York, NY: Harper Collins Publishers.

Goleman, Daniel. (1995). *Emotional Intelligence*. New York, NY: Bantam Books.

Idol, Lorna, & Jones, B.F. (Eds.). (1991). *Educational Values and Cognitive Instruction: Implications for Reform*. Hillsdale, NJ: Lawrence Erlbaum Associates.

Jones, B.F., Pierce, J., & Hunter, B. (1988). Teaching students to construct graphic representations. *Educational Leadership*. Volume 46. Number 4. pp. 20-25.

Marzano, Robert J., & Arredondo, Daisy. (1986). *Tactics for Thinking*. Aurora, CO: Mid Continent Regional Educational Laboratory.

Palinscar, A.S., & Brown, A.L. (1984). The reciprocal teaching of comprehension-fostering and comprehension-monitoring activities. *Cognition and Instruction*. Volume 1. Number 2. pp. 117-175.

Sharron, Howard, & Coulter, Martha. (1994). *Changing Children's Minds: Feuerstein's Revolution in the Teaching of Intelligence*. Exeter, Great Britain: BPC Wheatons Ltd.

Wolin, Steven J., & Wolin, Sybil. (1994). *The Resilient Self: How Survivors of Troubled Families Rise Above Adversity*. New York, NY: Villard Books.

District 220 teachers, Barrington, Illinois used the following resources:

Carr, Eileen, & Wilson, Karen K. *Guidelines for Evaluating Vocabulary Instruction.* Journal of Reading. Volume 29. Number 7.

Graves, Michael F., & Prenn, Maureen C. *Costs and Benefits of Various Methods of Teaching Vocabulary.* Journal of Reading. Volume 29. Number 7.

Nagy, William E. (1988). *Teaching Vocabulary to Improve Reading Comprehension.* NCTE.

Stahl, Steven A. (1990). *Beyond the Instrumentalist Hypothesis: Some Relationships Between Word Meanings and Comprehension.* University of Illinois at Champaign-Urbana.

Stahl, Steven A. *Principles of Effective Vocabulary Instruction.* Journal of Reading. Volume 29. Number 7.

aha! Process, Inc. • (800) 424-9484

Eye-openers at ...

Interested in more information?

We invite you to our website, www.ahaprocess.com to join our **aha!** News List!

Receive the latest income and poverty statistics free when you join! Then receive news, and updates every month!

Submit a new mental model – and receive Dr. Payne's latest article free!

Also on the website:

- Read success stories from our participants – from schools, social services, and businesses
- Three new workshops!
- An up-to-date listing of our books & videos
- Our convenient on-line store
- aha!'s training center schedule
- National Tour and Train the Trainer dates
- A videoclip of Dr. Payne
- News articles from around the country

    And more at ...

www.ahaprocess.com